A FIELD GUIDE
TO COLOR

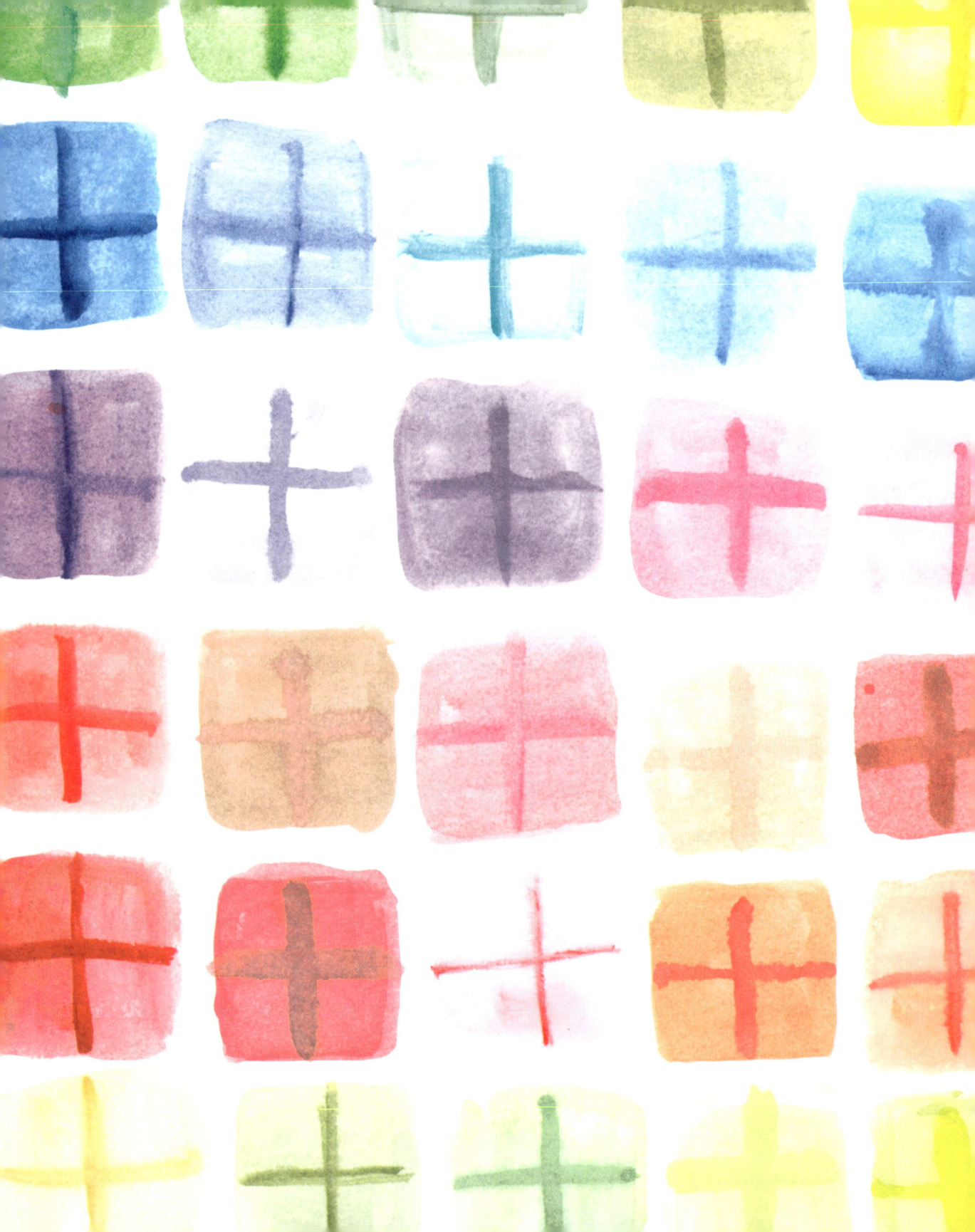

A FIELD GUIDE TO COLOR

A Watercolor Workbook

Lisa Solomon

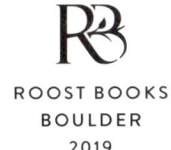

ROOST BOOKS
BOULDER
2019

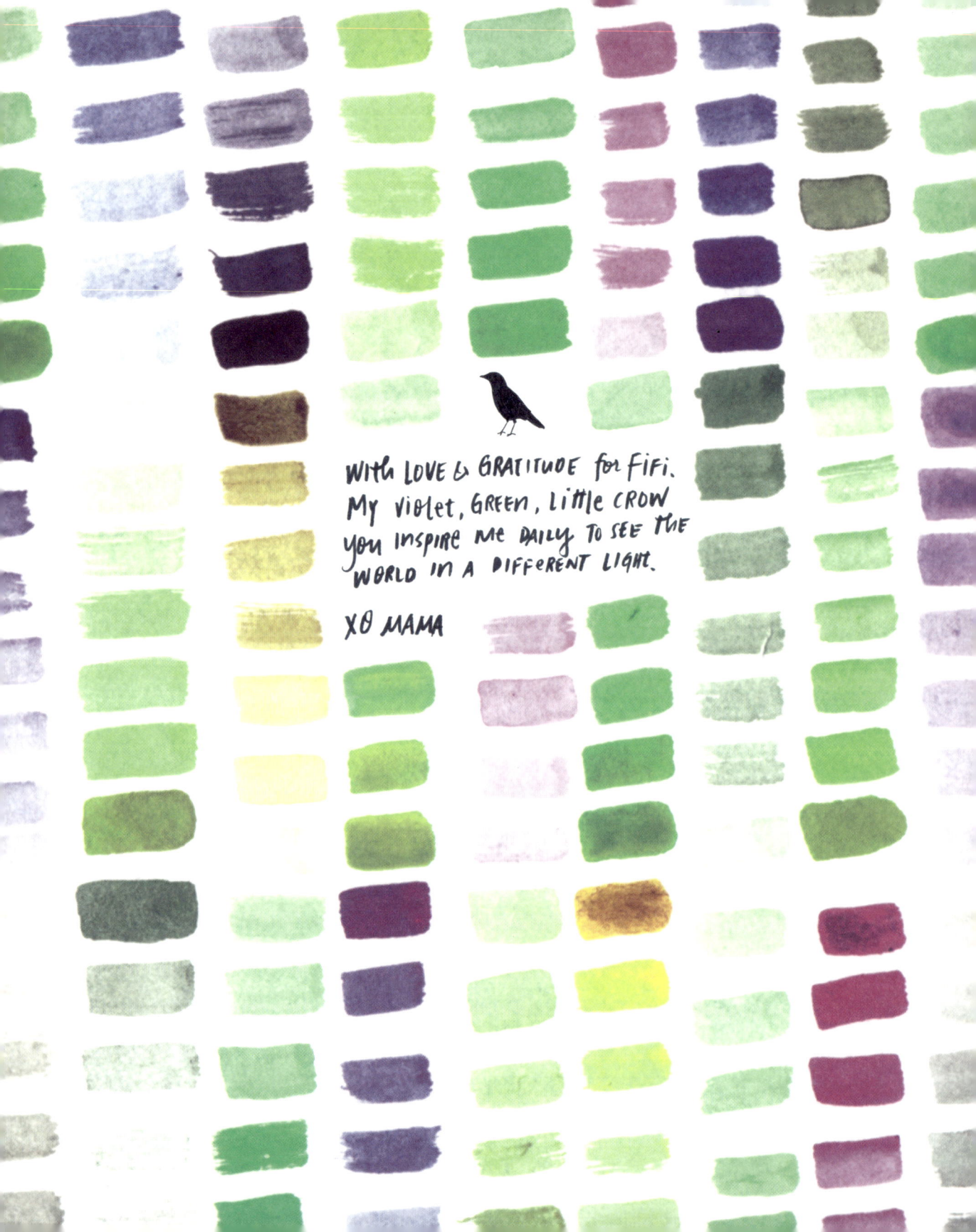

WITH LOVE & GRATITUDE for FIFI.
MY VIOLET, GREEN, LITTLE CROW
YOU INSPIRE ME DAILY TO SEE THE
WORLD IN A DIFFERENT LIGHT.

XO MAMA

HELLO, DEAR READER!

I'm so glad you are here. Welcome to the world of color! With this book, I'm inviting you to break out your paints, get messy, and work with your watercolors (or other water-based paint of your choice). In the coming pages you'll find a lot of space, prompts, and shapes to help you paint directly on the page. The idea is that you can read and work alongside my examples. But, I wanted to offer a word of warning. While we have worked to print this book on the best quality paper we can afford, sadly it is no substitute for watercolor paper. So, if you do choose to work right in the book, please know that the pages will cockle, buckle, and warp. The more water you use, the more likely this is going to happen. (Personally, I think the book will end up looking really cool with worn, used, and warped pages, but I don't want you to be surprised.) If you'd like to keep your book pristine, I encourage you to practice the exercises on watercolor paper.

If you're ready to turn this book into your own creative journal, let's go!

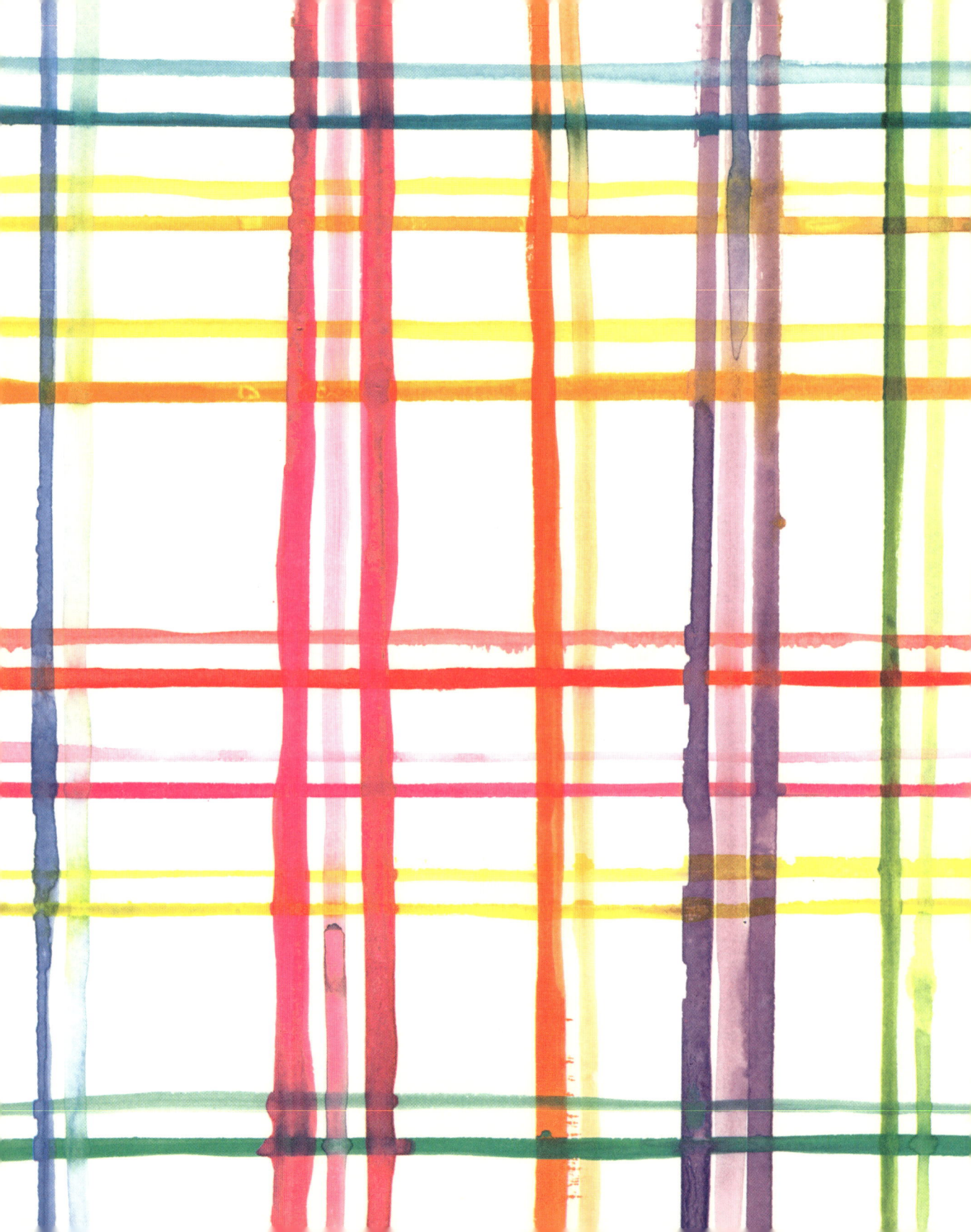

CONTENTS

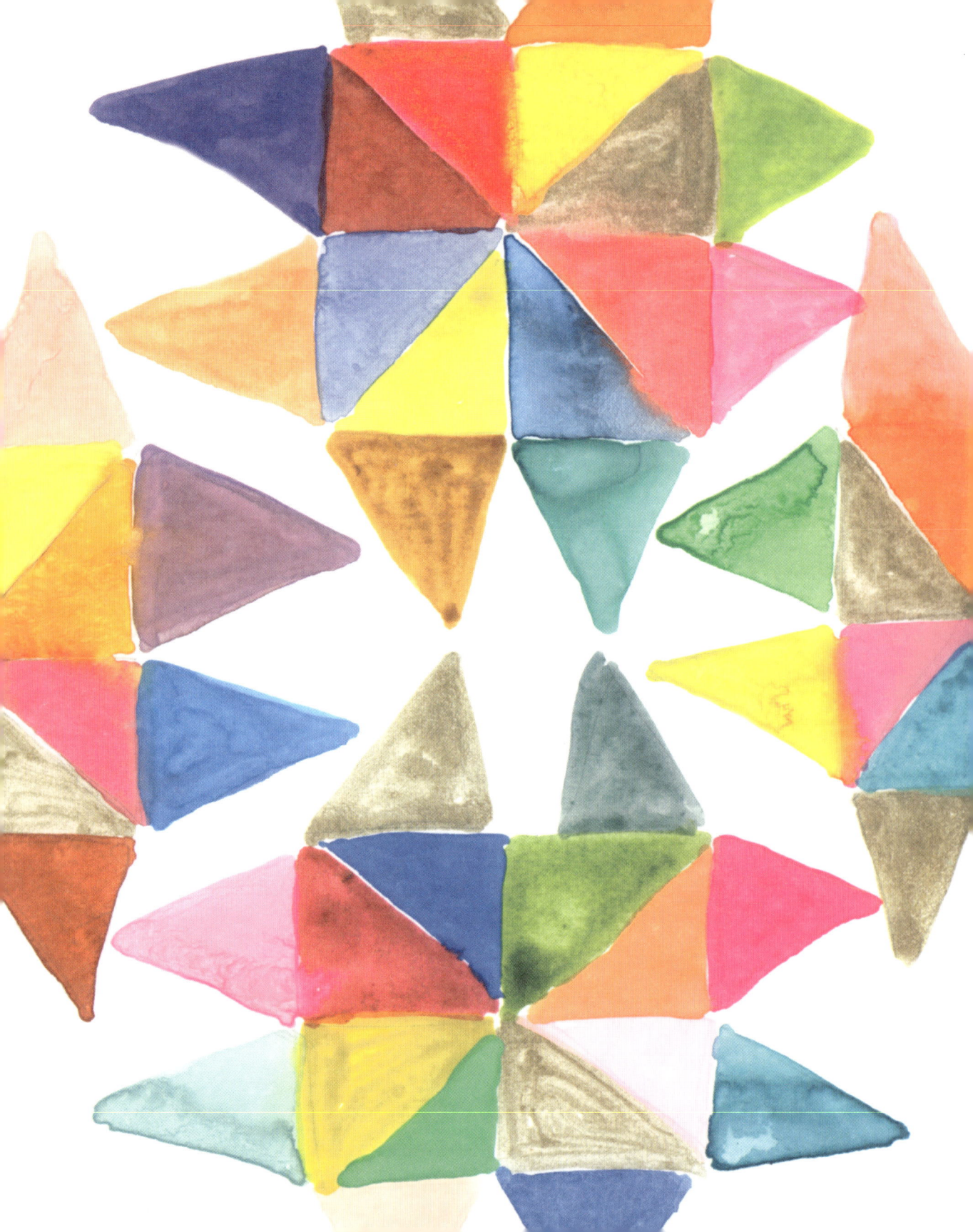

INTRODUCTION

I've always been fascinated by color. I can spend hours looking through Pantone books for the absolute "right" baby blue. I love just *looking* at lipsticks or markers or paints—soaking in the names of the colors, studying how they're all lined up, observing what happens when they're in a beautiful order or even out of order. (Would it be sad to admit that I've stood in stores rearranging mangled displays so they look better?) Colors make me feel and think and change my breathing. When I went to college and decided I was going to be an art major, I realized that I had some intuitive concepts of colors and how they worked. But as I painted (poorly) I realized I actually knew very little about how colors really worked, where they came from, and how to use them. The result was a *lot* of wasted paint.

Now as an artist and an art teacher, I've spent decades studying color, and I've read countless books on color theory (some of which are listed in the resources section). I've experimented with color in multiple media and in multiple ways. If you want to understand color, you need to immerse yourself in color. The way I use color has developed from time spent experimenting and by making lots and lots of mistakes. This book is the result of distilling *years* of my own experimentation with color.

The exercises that follow are meant to offer you a substantial introduction to color theory through *fun* and *playful* experiments. As you work your way through this book, a willingness to try things that might seem really, really wrong is key—which means not beating yourself up when things don't work out as you want. I try to keep the perspective that if I learned something, then the failure was completely worth it. I'm not saying this is easy, but try to keep it in mind as you work through all the exercises.

While the exercises offer directed lessons on color theory, the color meditations in between each lesson offer a time to pause and play with color. These "breaks" provide a wonderful counterpoint to the more traditional and challenging exercises. Over the last couple years, I got interested in meditation as a practice. I had a hard time finding a comfortable way to enter into it; I felt bombarded by all the "wellness" talk on "the Internets" and other media. But I slowly found a way to do it that felt comfortable to me. It involved regulating my breathing and feeling the breath go in through my nose, down to my belly, and back out through my nose; doing it when I could, even for a minute, even in the car when stuck in traffic (don't close your eyes while doing this); not feeling the need to sit forever or to allot a designated time; allowing my mind to wander and learning how to just acknowledge and let go of the thoughts that swirled in my brain. What I quickly realized was that I often get the same sensation and sense of well-being when I'm engrossed in the studio. In general, when I'm feeling stuck or unmotivated, or I don't have time to meditate in the "normal" way, I've found that doing a little painting makes all the difference in the world. I feel grounded and centered and ready to work. All the hustle-bustle and noise go away. I hope it does for you as well.

As I put my color meditations into practice, I found they were also a perfect warm-up exercise when I'm in the studio. Having some sort of routine or engagement with a repetitive project helps me grow as an artist. So what are color meditations? They're small watercolor paintings where I repeat the same shape or mark and simply adjust the color. The parameter of keeping the shape the same allows me to focus on just the color shifts. I try to use colors that I might not normally gravitate toward. I try to simply see what happens as I lay down one color next to the others. I try to experiment with the saturation of the colors, adding more or less water, adding a drop of another color and seeing how things shift. This practice has brought me an incredible amount of satisfaction and inspiration. And in all honesty, it continually teaches me new or surprising things about color.

For each color meditation in this book, make sure you set yourself up for success. Get out the paint you want to use; if it needs to be on a palette, put it in the order you'd like; get your water cups, paper towels, brushes, and so on at the ready and within reach. Perhaps you want an extra sheet of paper to use as a test sheet to try out colors, washes, brushstrokes, or saturations. If you are going to mix a lot of colors a nice clean palette helps. If you are new to painting, then try out different setups each time you do an exercise. Try placing your paint on the left or right or above your paper and try the same with your water. You'll soon develop a pattern or habit of setup that works best for you. Obviously I'm giving you some space in this book to create a color meditation for each prompt, but feel free to do more than one, and mix it up to learn more about different kinds of paper you own. You can use the same paints, just change the order, or not. Explore a huge range of color, or a narrow palette. *Remember, there's no right or wrong here.* Your meditation doesn't need to look like mine. In fact, I hope it doesn't. That said, if you feel too intimidated and really like mine, then by all means *copy* it. (Remember—say it with me—no right or wrong here. Make it your mantra.) Try to keep your feet planted. Try to not think of anything else but the mark and the colors you're choosing. Breathe in and out as you make your mark. Let your intuition run the show. *Please*—have fun!

My hope is that by trying the exercises and engaging with the meditations, you'll deepen your love and understanding of color—in whatever medium you choose to work in.

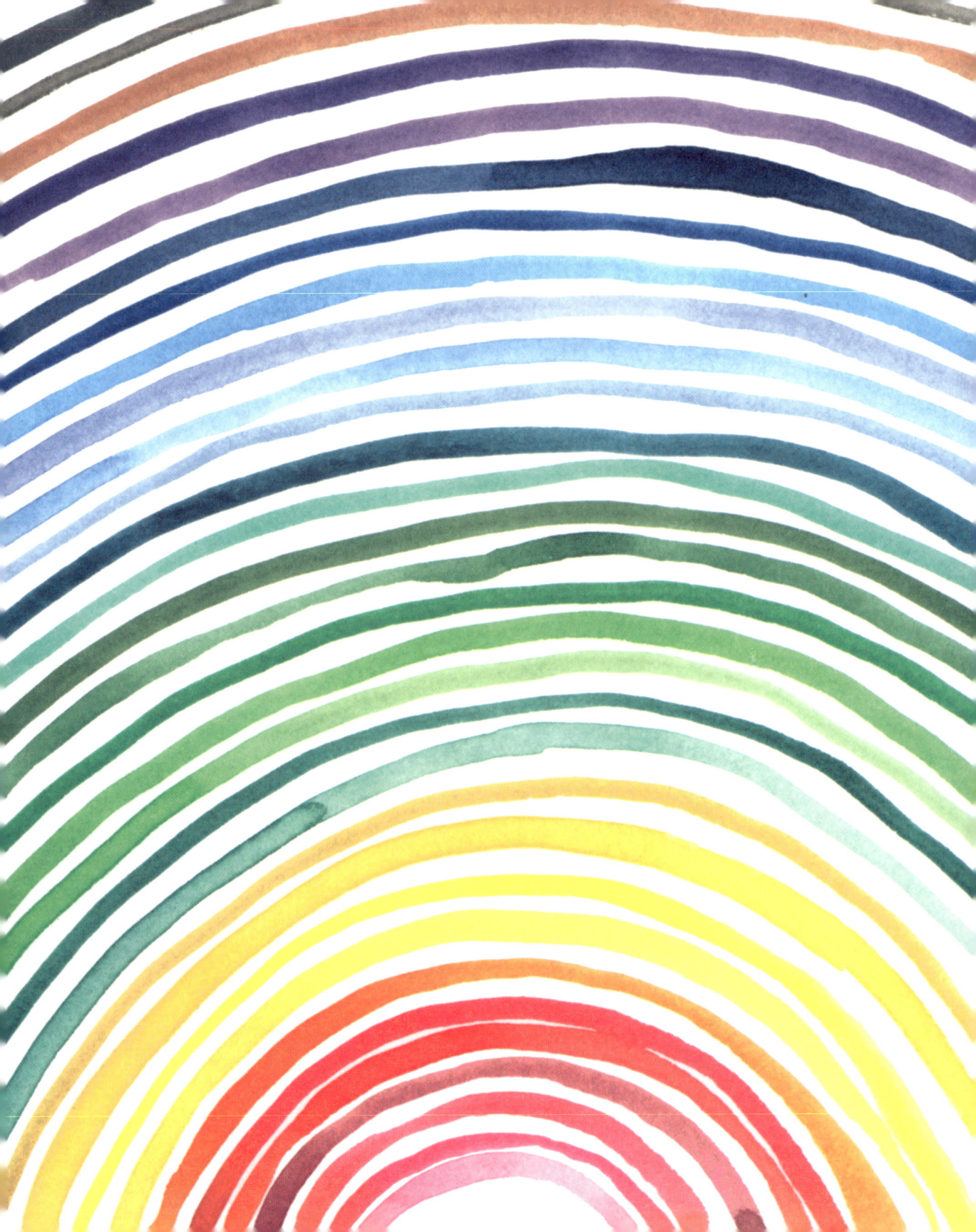

WHAT IS COLOR?

To understand color, it's helpful to have a sense of how we perceive color. In essence, color is all in our minds. It's highly personal and variable, influenced by the time of day, the type of light (artificial versus sun, direct versus indirect), the surrounding colors—you get the picture.

For example, imagine there's a green apple on the table. Why do we see it as green? There's light in the room. The light bounces back to our eyes. The green isn't *in* the apple. The apple is absorbing all the color wavelengths that our eyes can see and is reflecting green back to us. A white object is reflecting *all* the color waves back to us, and a black one is absorbing all the color waves.

When you really start to think about color, it becomes clear how very relational it is. If I say "red" to a room full of people, I can almost guarantee that everyone has a different red in their head. If I say "Coca-Cola red," and you've seen a Coke can, the red in our heads might be closer to matching. Color isn't only influenced by the time of day and the type of light, but also by the way our eyes and brains work and the culture we live in. We all perceive color differently, and we all have different cultural associations with color. For example, in China women wear red to weddings and white to funerals; in the United States it's white to weddings and black to funerals. And who decided that using pink for girls and blue for boys was a good idea? And how has culture pushed back against those gendered color ideas of late?

Colors can also bring out visceral reactions. Have you ever divided a room by who likes the color purple? Do it. It's pretty fun. Then subdivide—what kind of purple? Royal, lavender, magenta-tinged, blue-tinged … For whatever reason, purple tends to elicit some very strong reactions.

It's also interesting to explore the different ways we process color physically. Take the fascinating concept of afterimage, for example. In a nutshell, if you stare at an image of a bright red square in a bright green background for twenty to thirty seconds without blinking and then immediately look at a white wall or piece of paper, you'll see the opposite—a green square in a red background. There's also simultaneous contrast—how two different colors affect one another. We'll touch on this a bit in exercise 15 (page 125), but it's also something you could delve into deeper on your own. Similarly, optical mixing is another way we process color. Optical mixing explores how our eyes blend small areas or similar colors together to form a bigger picture or interpretation. (Impressionist paintings and mosaics are great examples of this.)

Welcome to the beautiful rabbit hole of color! I hope you find that having even a small sense of how we understand and talk about color is helpful as we move on to our color explorations.

TERMS
....

Let's go over some general terms that are part of the lexicon of color theory. (If you already know these, skip ahead.) Many of these will be developed further in upcoming exercises, so this is simply a quick rundown to familiarize yourself.

Hue. This is the name of the color itself—e.g., red, orange, blue.

Additive Color. This one used to confuse me to *no end*. This is when you're looking at the behavior of light mixtures. It helped me immensely to think about three light bulbs: a red, a green, and a blue one. If you overlap these you'll get familiar colors such as yellow (green + red) and purple (blue + red), but all three of them together will give you a white. It also helps me to think about these in terms of technology. Your TV and computer screens are RGB (red, green, blue) environments.

Subtractive Color. This is when you are looking at physical colors—paints, for example—and how they interact. This is basically what we're doing here in this book. You can also relate it to the printing process, which uses C (cyan), M (magenta), Y (yellow), K (black; it's *K* because we use *B* for blue in RGB). When you mix cyan with yellow you get green. Supposedly if you mix CMY you get K. (Try it. You'll see it's not usually what you think of as black.) Here's the tricky thing: your computer screen is RGB, but it's simulating a *subtractive* environment. Still with me? I know it's counterintuitive to think that subtractive = painting, but it is what it is. Paints (and most art supplies) use *pigments* or *colorants* that determine the colors we see.

Warm Colors. These are generally thought of as what you see in daylight (or sunrise/sunsets). You've got your reds, yellows, oranges, and browns.

Cool Colors. These are generally nighttime colors—your blues, greens, grays. But here's the thing: every *hue* (white, black, red, etc.) can lean one way or the other. We often talk about a cool white (more blue) versus a warm one (more yellow), and this is true of *any* hue we can see and create. Warm and cool are helpful descriptors.

Lightness/Darkness or Tints/Shades. This is how light or dark a hue is; it relates to how much white or black has been added to each hue. This isn't saturation, which is the relative intensity of a color. I like to think of saturation as how much you can *see* through a color—think *opacity* on your computer screen, from 100 percent (full strength of the color) to 10 percent.

Value. This is another way to talk about the relative lightness or darkness of the hue. If you think in terms of black and white, black is at one end of your spectrum, white is at the other, and there are all the values of gray in between. Things can be different *hues* and be the same *value*—for example a very dark red is similar in value to a very dark gray. Value can be used to harmonize or create big contrasts. One way to help check the values of hues is to use a program such as Photoshop to turn your image black and white. In doing so you can determine if what you've made has a good range of value or if the overall values you used are similar. You can also squint—things that are relative in lightness and darkness will consolidate as you do so.

There will be more terms that pop up as we work through the exercises in the book.

COLOR SYSTEMS

To make more sense of color, there are, in general, different identified *gamuts* (ranges or scopes) or *color systems*. As you begin to study color, it's good to have some familiarity with these. Here are a few of the systems that are most frequently used.

RGB (Red, Green, Blue). This *additive* color spectrum combines those three colors of light on a spectrum of 255 to create the colors we see (the most familiar application of this is on your computer or TV screen). In RGB, black is R-0, G-0, B-0 and white is R-255, G-255, B-255.

CMYK (Cyan, Magenta, Yellow, Black). This is the spectrum used for physical printing. It's a smaller gamut, aka has fewer colors in it, than RGB—if you've ever printed something from the computer and it looked one way on screen and another way printed, this is why. There are websites and Pantone books that offer formulas to convert colors you see on-screen into CMYK so that you won't be surprised. In CMYK, black is C-0, M-0, Y-0, K-100 and a standard green is C-100, M-0, Y-100, K-0. If you wanted your green to be darker you could add K or some M.

HEX Colors. These are often referred to as web colors, although these days there are places that use them to print (such as onto fabric). They're made up of three sets of two numbers or letters starting from 00 and ending with FF. Black is #000000, a standard red is #FF0000, white is #FFFFFF.

PMS/Pantone Matching System. This is a commercial color system that has slowly but surely become world famous. Each year Pantone releases a color of the year and a color trend forecast. If you want to be sure that something in print will be a specific color, then Pantone is the way to go. They sell specific ink colors (for digital printing, silk-screening, letterpress, etc.), and these days they also have an app, several books, colored pencils, and a gazillion other things with their brand.

Our eyes see millions of colors but understanding and utilizing color systems will allow you and someone else to agree on what color you're using or talking about.

PAINTS, BRUSHES, AND OTHER MATERIALS

This book is designed for you to work on these pages alongside my prompts. There are some basic materials that you'll need (unless you can magically make art appear by waving your hand). If you're already an artist/maker, you may be well stocked and ready to go. If you've got some paints and brushes that you like and know how to use, paper towels and cups for water, you can just go ahead and skip to the first exercise. But if you're brand-spanking-new to painting (to be honest, I'm a bit jealous if you are because—how fun!), or if you want an overview of recommended items, here's what I think you need to get the most out of this book.

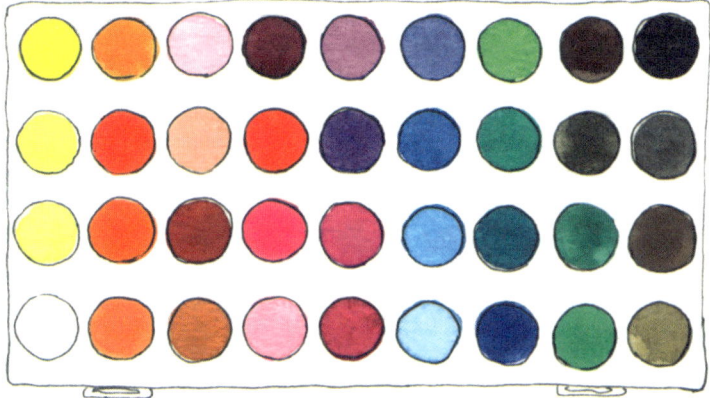

PAINT

For the projects in this book, I recommend using watercolor or gouache in either a tube or pans. (And you can mix these together—both the tube/pan and watercolor/gouache. It's like one big happy family.) For the record, both these paints use the same pigments and binder (gum arabic). There are either

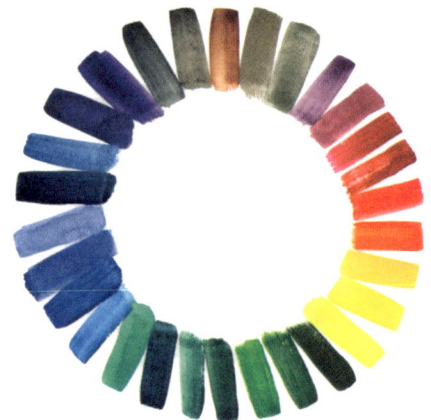

more/bigger pigment flakes used in gouache *and/or* they add a chalk to it that ultimately makes it more opaque—that's really the major difference between the two.

You could certainly use bottled inks or acrylic paints of any kind if that's what you have. I really recommend *water-based* media because it's so much easier to clean up and easier to control in terms of saturation—you just add more water to make them more transparent. And it won't ruin your paper. Oil-based media will seep, leaving a stain on your paper and eventually could eat through the page leaving a hole. With acrylic paint you really need to use mediums to get them to work correctly, and they dry out if you leave them on a palette. You can also leave tube watercolors/gouaches out and rewet to reuse! (Bonus!)

I recommend getting the biggest set of watercolors/gouache you can afford, but you can easily do almost all the exercises with a bare-bones set of red, blue, yellow, white, black, and brown. (I say "almost" because the color-matching exercises

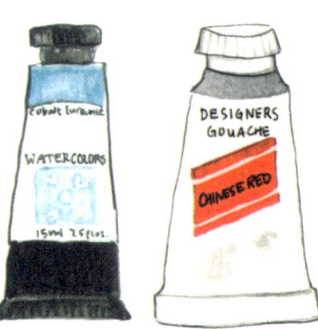

will be harder with a very small set.) Some things to keep in mind: different types of blues and reds will give you very different kinds of purples; some colors lean warm, some lean cool, and these will affect how your colors mix.

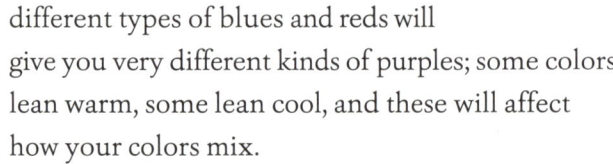

First I'll explain what I use, and then I'll offer a couple of alternatives.

I use a set of thirty-six Kuretake watercolor pans. They use Japanese characters for their color names, but they also use numbers. They also offer sets in different sizes; their twelve-color set would be a lovely way to start.

I also have a set of twenty-four Winsor & Newton pans, which includes:

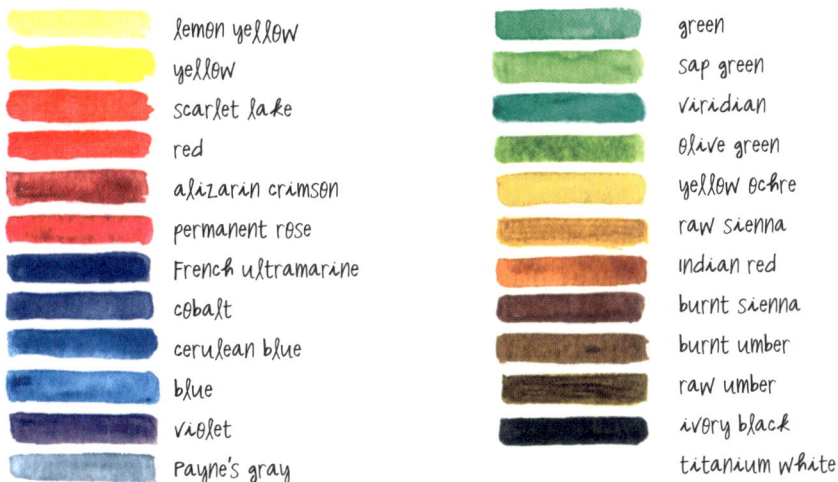

lemon yellow
yellow
scarlet lake
red
alizarin crimson
permanent rose
French ultramarine
cobalt
cerulean blue
blue
violet
Payne's gray

green
sap green
viridian
olive green
yellow ochre
raw sienna
indian red
burnt sienna
burnt umber
raw umber
ivory black
titanium white

I've augmented this set with:

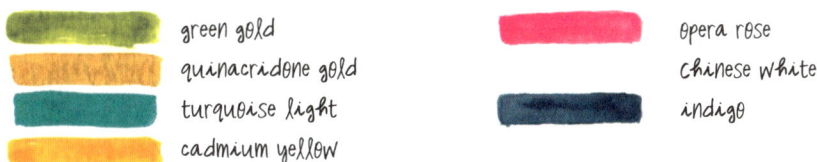

green gold
quinacridone gold
turquoise light
cadmium yellow

opera rose
chinese white
indigo

I keep additional tubes of lamp black, Mars black, and zinc white.

I also really love my incredibly inexpensive thirty-six pan set of Artist's Loft watercolors (no names of colors anywhere, and not the most pigmented, but still lovely).

Finally, I have a set of random gouaches that I often mix and use with my watercolors to make them less transparent or shift their hue.

If you're starting from scratch and want to build your own set, these are the basic twelve colors to begin with. Because brands sometimes name colors differently, please note I sometimes list several options/names for each hue (you don't need to get four kinds of warm yellow–just one):

titanium white

ivory black

yellow – Hansa yellow, Winsor yellow, azo

warm yellow – quinacridone gold, Hansa yellow deep, Indian yellow, chrome yellow deep

scarlet – pyrrol scarlet, Winsor red, vermillion

crimson – alizarin crimson, carmine, quinacridone crimson (this is a type of synthetic pigment, and it comes in different colorways, which is why there's a gold and a crimson and other quinacridone colors as well.)

rose – permanent rose, quinacridone rose

ultramarine blue – this is pretty much the same name across all brands; sometimes it's called French ultramarine

cerulean – same; it's pretty much the same across brands

phthalo blue (green shade) – Winsor blue, Prussian blue

phthalo green (blue shade) – Windsor green

yellow ochre – goethite, transparent yellow oxide

burnt sienna or burnt orange – same across all brands

raw or burnt umber – same across all brands; Indian red is a good substitute

I really recommend sticking with one set of paint–large or small–throughout all these exercises. You'll definitely learn more this way. You can always do the exercises again in another media or with another set of colors at any point in time, but I promise you'll get the most bang for your buck if you approach these projects with the same color set.

If you've never worked with water-based media, spend a little bit of time just fooling around on a scrap of heavyweight watercolor paper (if you use printer paper you will not be happy). There are all kinds out there–there's a bit more about paper in the next section. Try using the least amount of water you can with the paint, then add a *lot* more water and see what happens.

Blot your brush and see what happens. Wet the paper first and put your brush into that wet spot and see what happens (this is a *wet-on-wet* application). How long of a stroke can you make before your brush stops making a mark? Just get a feel for how the paint works and moves.

If you really want to geek out about colors, here's a tip: Each tube or pan should be labeled with a pigment number. (It's *tiny*, and on the back; on some pans it's on the packaging. FYI many inexpensive brands DO NOT list pigments.) For example, quinacridone rose is PV19. Any tube of paint that uses that pigment will list PV19. Some brands mix pigments and then label them with names, some of which might seem familiar. For example, phthalo turquoise might have phthalo blue's pigment, PB15, in addition to others. It won't look or act the same as straight phthalo blue. The great thing about looking at pigment colors is that these codes can help guide you across all brands. If you know you like Indian yellow with NY20 in it, any brand with that pigment should be consistent in color. Also, if you're mixing colors, note that the more pigments involved, the more chance your colors will get muddy. This is because you think you're mixing two colors, but if there are actually four pigments in one tube and three in another you're actually mixing *seven* colors!

PAPER

Let's chat about paper for a second, shall we? Although this book provides you space to try all these exercises out right here, I'm hoping that you'll like them so much you'll want to do them again. After all, repetition is really what leads to breakthroughs and mastery of craft (in my opinion, anyway). Plus, I'm really hoping that the color meditations will take over your life and you'll end up with stacks and stacks of them—and if that's the case, you'll need a lot of paper!

With wet media it's really important to use the right kind of paper. Have you ever tried to paint with watercolors on laser printer paper? It usually leads to a buckling, pilled, potentially holey mess. Even regular sketchbook paper won't hold up to pass after pass of gouache.

There are two traditional types of paper: hot press and cold press. Hot press is smooth and allows for more details, but the surface *can* buckle if you keep layering your paint. Cold press is bumpy and textural–allowing water to soak into it, but cold press *can* be a bit unpredictable because there are literally divots and thus the paint might not travel in a straight line. These days there are also synthetic papers (such as Yupo or Dura-Lar) that are more like vellums but accept wet media. They offer a completely different look and feel and they're semiopaque (which I *love*). Traditional rice or mulberry papers are an option as well; they're surprisingly durable for how fragile they seem. Paint tends to spread on them, though, so keep that in mind. (This means your tiny dot might become a medium dot on its own.) There are now also a whole host of mixed-media papers that work fairly well with wet media. When in doubt, read the package; it usually says what the intended media is.

Papers come in different weights: 90 lb. (190 gsm), 140 lb. (300 gsm), 260 lb. (356 gsm), 300 lb. (636 gsm)–more weight equals thicker paper. Many think that papers under 260 lb. should be stretched to keep them flat. (This is a process where you wet and tape the paper down so it lies flat and doesn't buckle as you work. You can google how to do this if it interests you.) Papers also vary by manufacturer and price–try different kinds to see what you like. Paper comes in single sheets, in packs, or on blocks–in *so many* sizes–with and without deckled (torn-looking/textured) edges. A lot of people like blocks because they offer stability (no need to stretch the paper). I tend to have a variety in my stash: a less expensive pad to try out washes and ideas, and more expensive paper for when I'm really getting into something. People can get very, very picky and personal about what they use and why, but if you don't have a preference, you're in the beautiful position of finding what works best for you! Note that you'll get the best results if you work on watercolor paper, but the paper in the book will get you started. (Keep in mind, however, that these pages will warp.)

BRUSHES

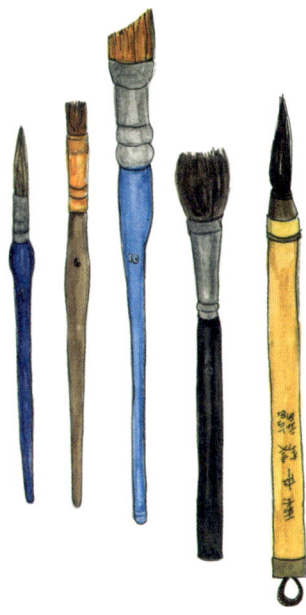

Oh, there are *so* many brushes!

Real hair brushes, like sable, are the best for watercolor/gouache, but these days synthetics are catching up, and they actually work better for acrylics.

I also *love* Asian bamboo and sumi brushes because they work really well, they can create very fine lines and also fill big shapes, and they're relatively inexpensive.

Here's a quick rundown of types of brushes that will work well for the exercises here (and what I used in preparing the samples). Brushes come in tiny sizes, from 000 to very, very big 50+, and are also sometimes marked by inches, such as ⅜ inch to 2 inches. *Use brushes you like the feel of* and screw the rules and conventions, I always say.

This book is small, so I would stick with brushes that you can fit into the shapes on the pages. If you don't have any brushes, then a good variety pack will give you a range of sizes and styles to experiment with.

Round. These come to a point. They're really good for fine lines, small spaces, and details. They also can provide long, even line-like strokes. Sizes 0–4 would be good for this book.

Flat. These have medium to long hairs that end in a square, blunt edge. They come in different widths. They're good for maneuverability, the wider ones for creating washes; if you turn them on their sides the edge can do some line work too. I think any size of flats would be useful, but I used 0–6.

Angular/Angled. This is my current favorite go-to brush shape. The small point is really great for detailing and getting into corners, and you can use it like a flat, too, to fill spaces. It's super versatile. For some reason, angled brushes often list an inch width, not just a size. A 6, 8, or 12 would work well, aka ¼ inch, ⅜ inch, ½ inch.

Traditional Bamboo/Calligraphy. These are usually goat hair (which definitely feels/works differently than sable)—their long point allows for strokes that vary from wide to fine in one motion (not every brush can do this). Any size from 1 to 6 would be useful in this book. They're also wonderful if you want to practice hand lettering.

Mop/Oval Wash. Mops usually have a point; ovals don't. Both are great for laying down big washes or swaths of color. They're not very practical for this book except for maybe color meditations, but ...

Hake/Mottlers/Squares. These are usually bigger than the other brushes described above. Hake is a traditional Asian brush often used to prewet paper or lay down a first wash. Mottlers usually have short handles but work in the same way. Squares are just larger versions of flats that are shaped more like a square than a rectangle.

PAPER TOWELS/BLOT CLOTH

If you're using watercolor/gouache, you'll need paper towels or a nice and sturdy cotton cloth to blot your brushes with. I like to use old baby burp cloths or cut pieces of t-shirts (higher end, not too thin). I tend to gravitate toward white cloths so I can see where clean areas are. Clean areas are useful for freshly blotting pools of paint or cleaning up a color on your palette. Watercolor and gouache are fairly washable, so I tend to throw them in laundry now and again too. Try to avoid using something that will shed lint onto your brush. The lint will transfer to your paper and make smooth washes impossible.

PALETTE

My all-time favorite palette is the enamel-coated one. It's white with a lip so the water doesn't run off the end. If you're using paints out of a tube you can line them up along the sides and use the inside area for mixing. There are also some great plastic or ceramic white palettes of all shapes and sizes. Many sets of watercolors in pans provide a white palette area to mix. I suggest using a white or neutral gray palette so you can really see your colors, but you could always use a dinner plate or piece of glass (tape the edges, please!) just as easily. Keep in mind that something with a lip or edge will most likely work best because you're using water ... it has a tendency to run a bit wild.

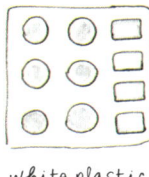
white plastic

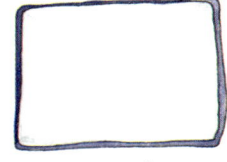
enamel

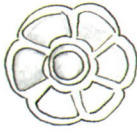
ceramic

If you choose to use acrylic paints, you might need a few more supplies. You'll need a palette knife, because mixing paints with your brushes is the fastest way to ruin them. You'll also need some mediums. Do *not* try to paint acrylics with just water. I promise you will be frustrated. Immediately. You'll need some matte or gloss medium to put in your paint. I also really recommend a flow aid (this is something you drop into your water for acrylic), and then a glazing or pouring medium to thin out your paint so it can be transparent. There's a lot of info online about acrylic painting (I teach a class on Creativebug about it), and I suggest you watch or read a few things, and play around to get comfortable before you attempt the exercises in this book.

A NOTE ON COST

Before we dive in, I want to take a minute to say, with regard to materials, *you get what you pay for!* This is just a truth in art supplies. In paint, the more expensive paints contain better pigments and more of them. Cheaper brands use chalk and other fillers. With brushes, the natural hair brushes will hold water beautifully and keep their points for years and years to come if you take care of them. Cheaper brushes will fall apart or not hold their shapes. Expensive paper will take abuse—you can apply layers of washes and it won't buckle or tear. Cheap paper will tear, buckle, or fall apart. That said, I'm not really a materials snob. I love my cheap five-dollar watercolor palette as much as my eleven-dollar tube of paint. They just perform differently, and I don't expect them to do the same things. Same with my brushes. I have synthetics that I travel with, or stuff into bags, or use for practice, or tests, or to create textures (I don't want to push down hard with my fifty-dollar brush). But I adore my real sables because they do things that the cheap brushes don't. Please just keep that in mind. Cost shouldn't really be a barrier, and you can definitely make gorgeous things with inexpensive supplies, but I want you to know there is a difference (and you'll learn this quickly if you do your own comparisons).

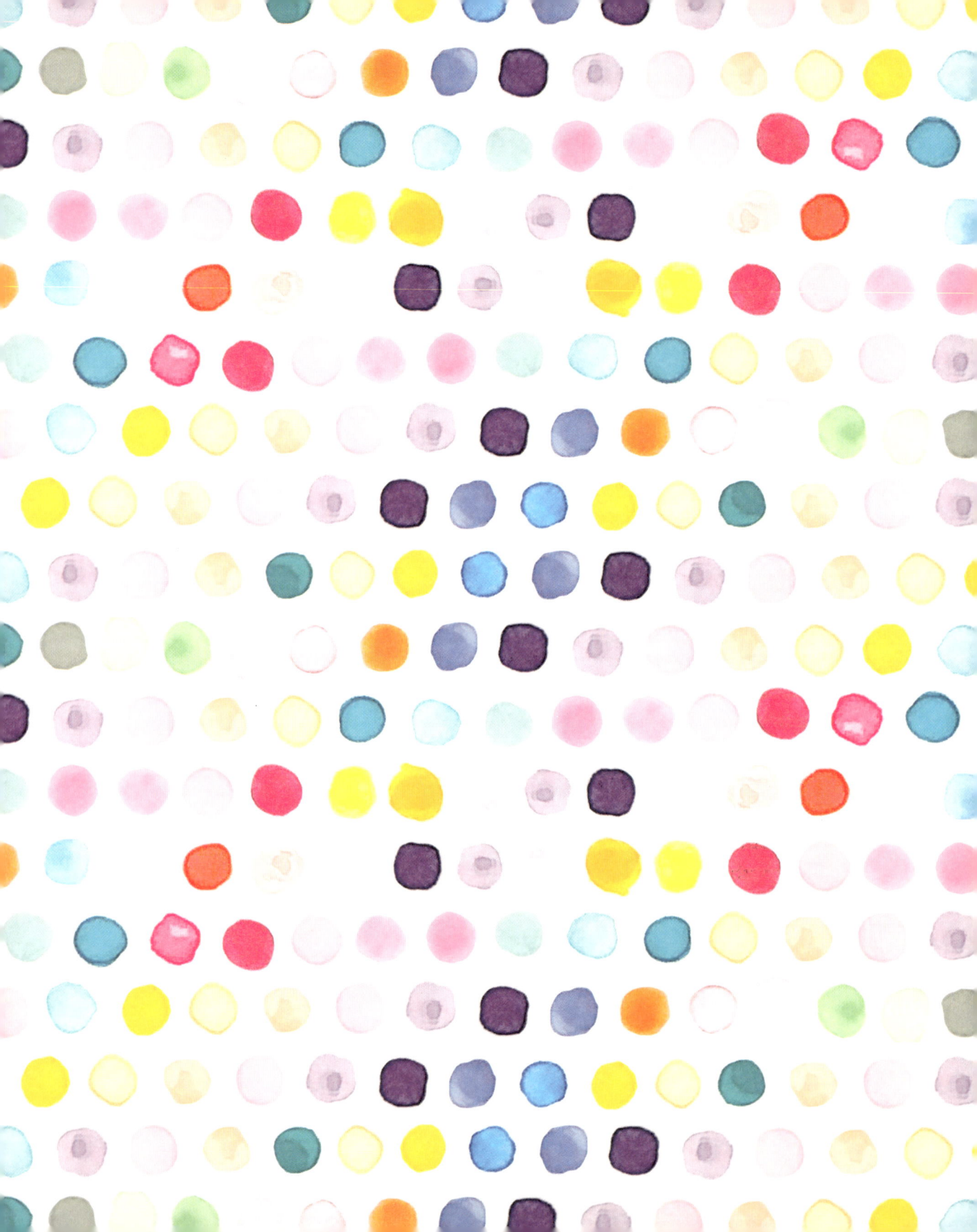

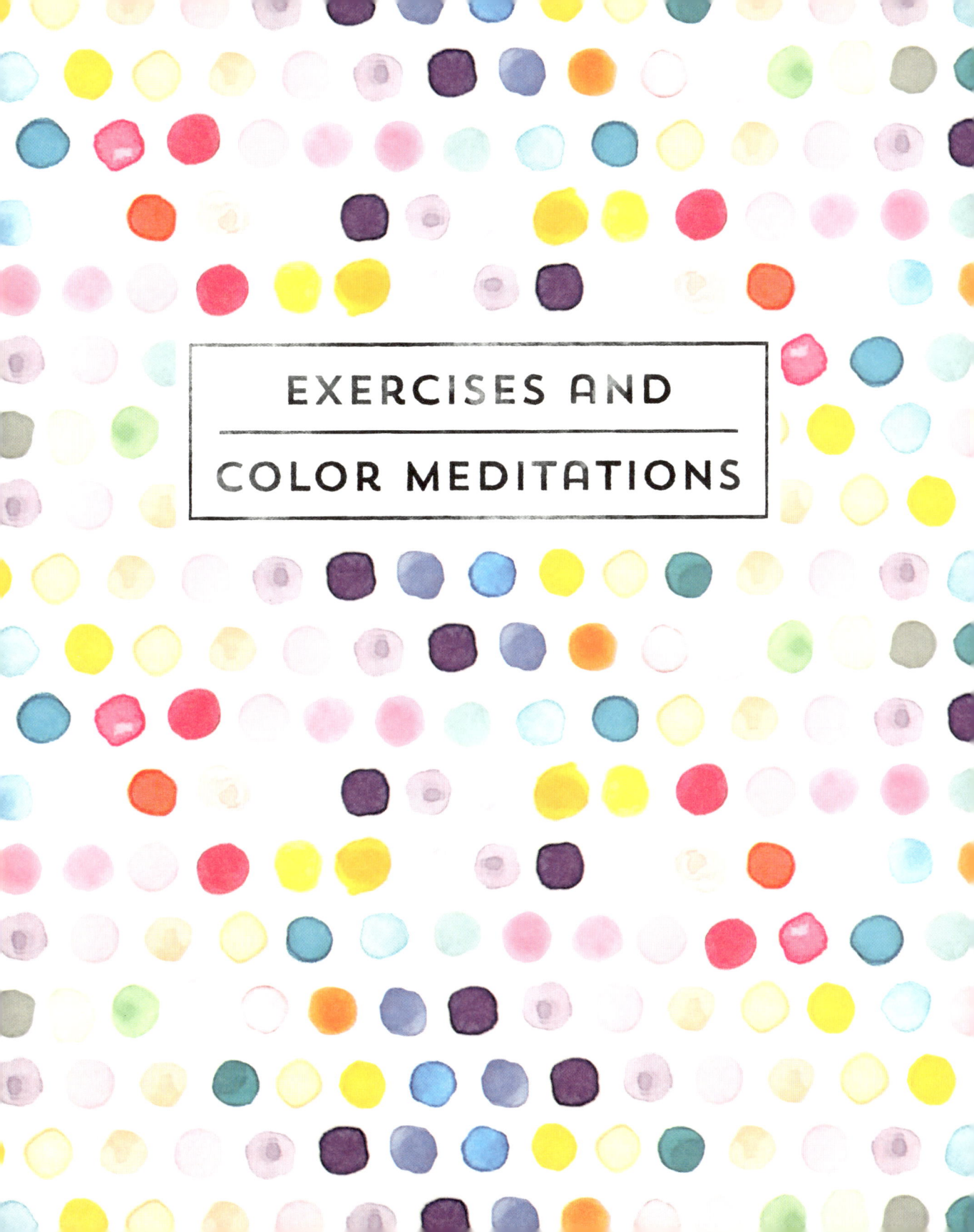

EXERCISES AND
COLOR MEDITATIONS

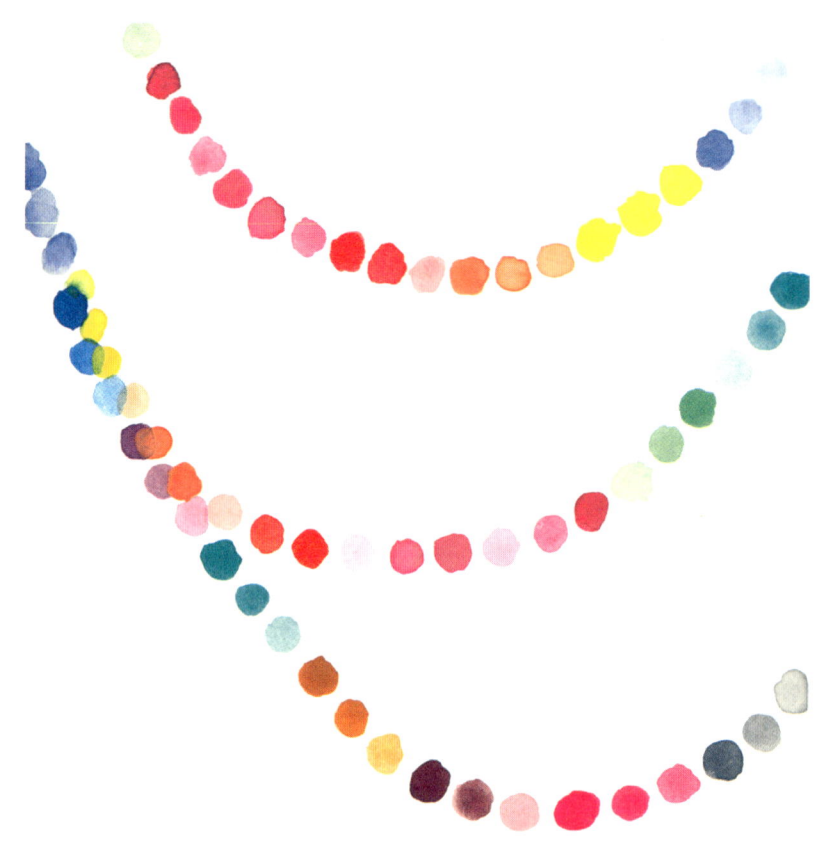

Color Meditation | **DOTS**

Let's warm up with our very first color meditation!

My first-ever color meditation was dots. I was thinking about garlands, so I painted dots, shifting the color saturation for each one along a swooping line. Each color got three dots: full strength, half strength, quarter strength (aka saturation shift).

So let's start with *dots*. You can do them in garlands, in rows, randomly all over the page. They can overlap or not touch; they can be big, small, all the same size, increase or decrease in size. They can be made with a big brush, a small brush, a stick, a dropper. Just make some dots.

▸ Paint some dots

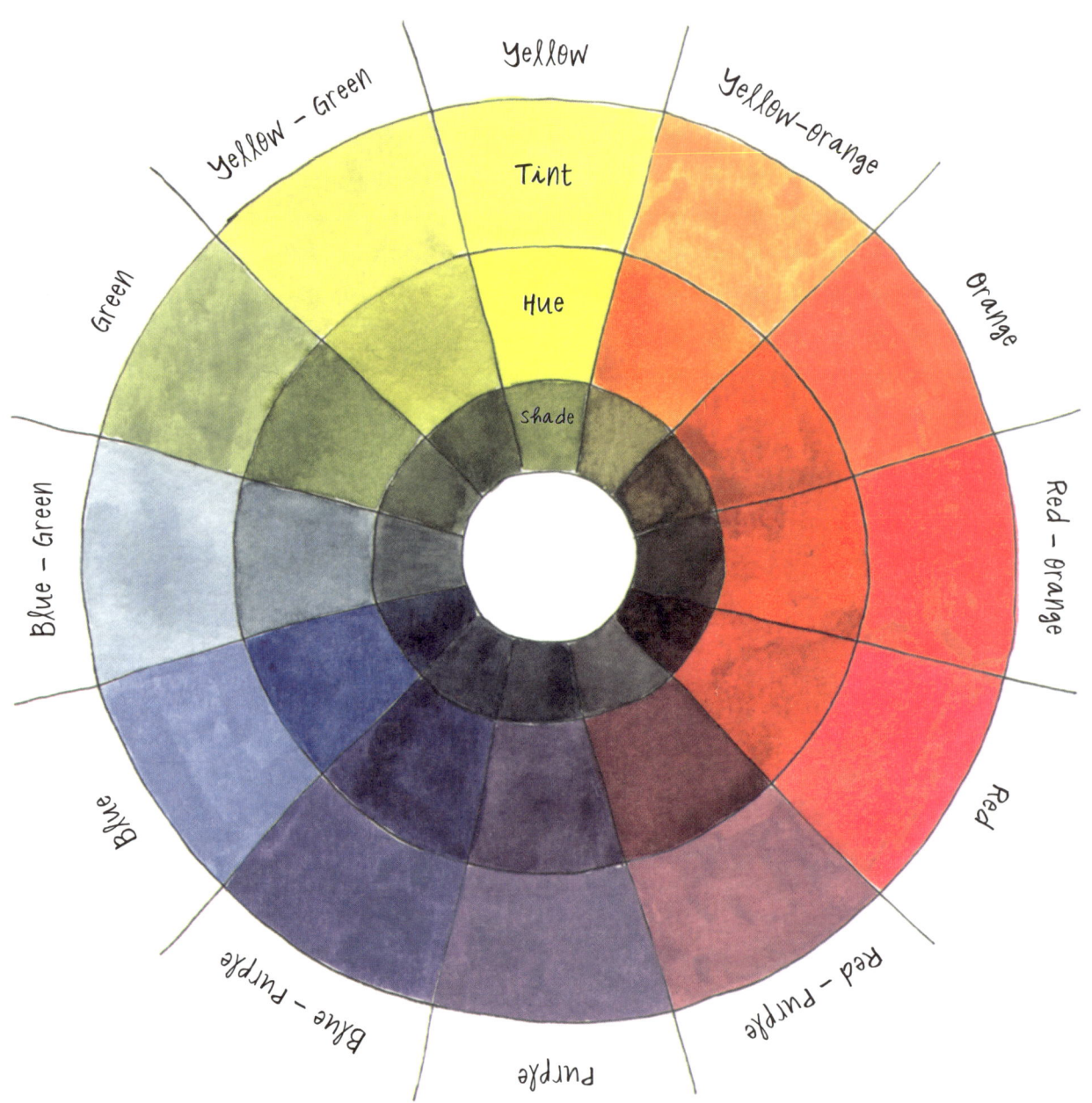

1.

MAKE A TRADITIONAL COLOR WHEEL WITH TINTS AND SHADES

If you've taken any art courses over the years you were probably assigned a color wheel. (If you hated it, go ahead and groan now.) Maybe you really enjoyed it. (I admit that I did, but I've always been a color geek.) Here's the thing, though: Did you really think about what a color wheel actually does for you? Why you might want to make one? What it actually has to teach you?

I truly believe that there's more freedom and space to break rules and create your own ways of working if you have a good grasp on what is often considered the science of color. Making a color wheel is an easy way for you to not only intellectually consider what happens when you mush colors together but to also feel and see how colors blend and relate to one another. *But* if starting out with this traditional color wheel just makes your stomach drop, skip it for now. Please move on to the next exercise where you get to make your very own color wheel, which should be much more fun.

If you're still with me, let's tackle this thing. A color wheel is a great starting point, right? Remember what it's based on? The primary colors. Summon your inner child and say them with me: red, yellow, blue. Supposedly we can make almost all the colors of the world with these three colors. OK, maybe that's true, but it can be really, really hard. So the first thing I want you to do is *decide that this color wheel is not going to be perfect*. It doesn't need to be a masterpiece. In fact, you'll learn more if it's kind of ugly. I can almost guarantee your purple is going to be ugly—or at least not what you envision as purple. That's what we want. Because when we make these kinds of "mistakes," we're learning.

Let's make a twelve-step color wheel with tints and shades.

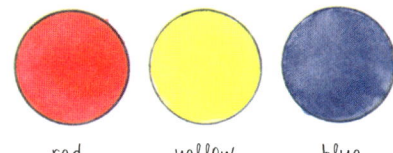

red   yellow   blue

Start by filling in your primaries. Use your gut to determine the best primaries to use. A good red doesn't have too much orange and isn't too crimson.

Next, we'll make all the hues and their tints and shades. What are tints and shades, you ask? A *tint* is when you take your *hue* (the color) and add it to white. A *shade* is when you take your *hue* and add black. For the purposes of this prompt, let's try to add about the same amount of your hue to the same amount of white or black every time. It might be easiest if you actually set out twelve globs of white that are the same size so that you're ready to go when you tackle the tints.

There are a couple ways to approach filling in your color wheel. You can make all your tints and shades while you work your way around the color wheel—I do this because I like to work while the colors are fresh and still wet. (Especially if you're working with acrylics, there's the danger that your paints will dry out before you get back to them.) Alternatively, you can make all the *hues* first and then get to the *tints* and *shades* later. Just keep track of all the hue locations on your palette. Do what feels right to you. There's no law that says you have to go in a certain order—or even start with a certain color. Feel free to do this at your own pace, or you can work around with me.

Secondaries

orange

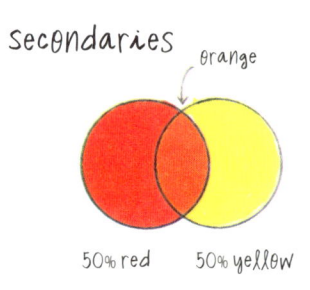

50% red   50% yellow

Tertiaries

yellow orange

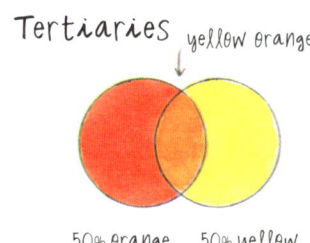

50% orange   50% yellow

After the primaries, you'll make secondaries. Take a dollop of red and a dollop of yellow the same size. Mix. Fill in your orange slot. This is a secondary color or other hue. Take that orange and mix a dollop with the same size dollop of yellow and then of red. You'll now have yellow-orange and red-orange. These are tertiary colors. (*Do not* be alarmed if your red-orange is close to either the red or the orange. Remember we're learning about how these paints work.) If you run out of your orange, make some more (with the same size dollops you started with). Now is a good time to take all these warm *hues* you've made and create your *tints* and *shades*. Be consistent in the amount of white and black you mix with your hues.

Now take your primary yellow and blue and follow the same process. You've got some greens and turquoises, right? Here's the fun part. Take your red and blue and make a purple. And you get ... not what most of us envision as *purple*, right? It's a bit darker and muddier? Yeah. That's because it's way easier to make a purple with a crimson (such as alizarin or quinacridone) and a not-so-bright-blue blue (such as a phthalo or Prussian). Of course, you can always buy a purple you like, and I encourage you to do so, but through this process you actually *know* more about the color purple, right?

Continue on making all your secondary and tertiary hues and their corresponding tints and shades.

So what is all this for, anyway? Well, a color wheel is helpful in understanding color families and relationships. And we'll be exploring some of those in exercise 3 (page 39).

PRO TIP: If you are using the same brush as you work your way around the color wheel, make sure to rinse it out thoroughly and use a clean cloth to blot it clean. Even a small amount of leftover paint from another color could easily contaminate your next color. If you have the option of using more than one brush, I find it most helpful to use a separate brush for the tints so your white in particular stays very clean and bright.

Practice mixing your colors in even ratios here before you move onto your color wheel.

secondaries = 50/50 mix of your primaries

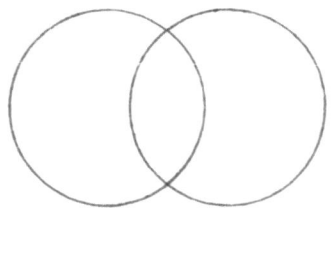 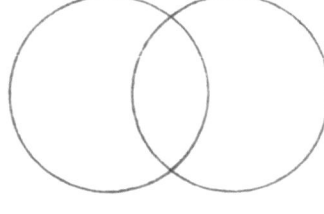

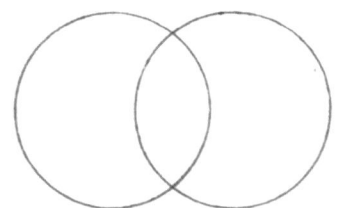 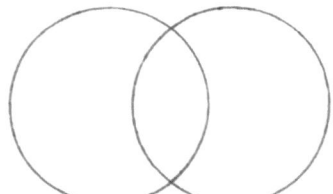

tertiaries = 50/50 mix of your secondaries

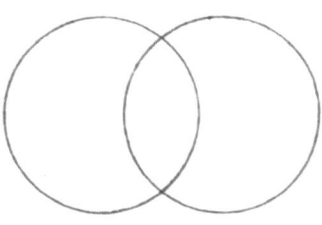 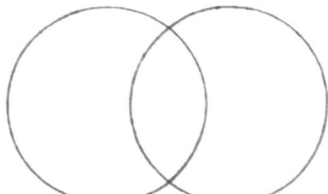

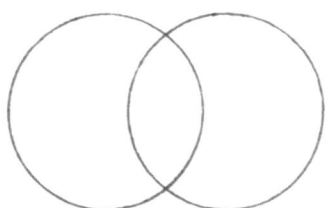 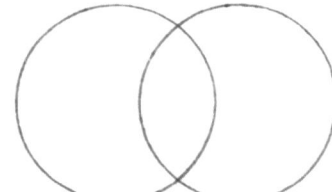

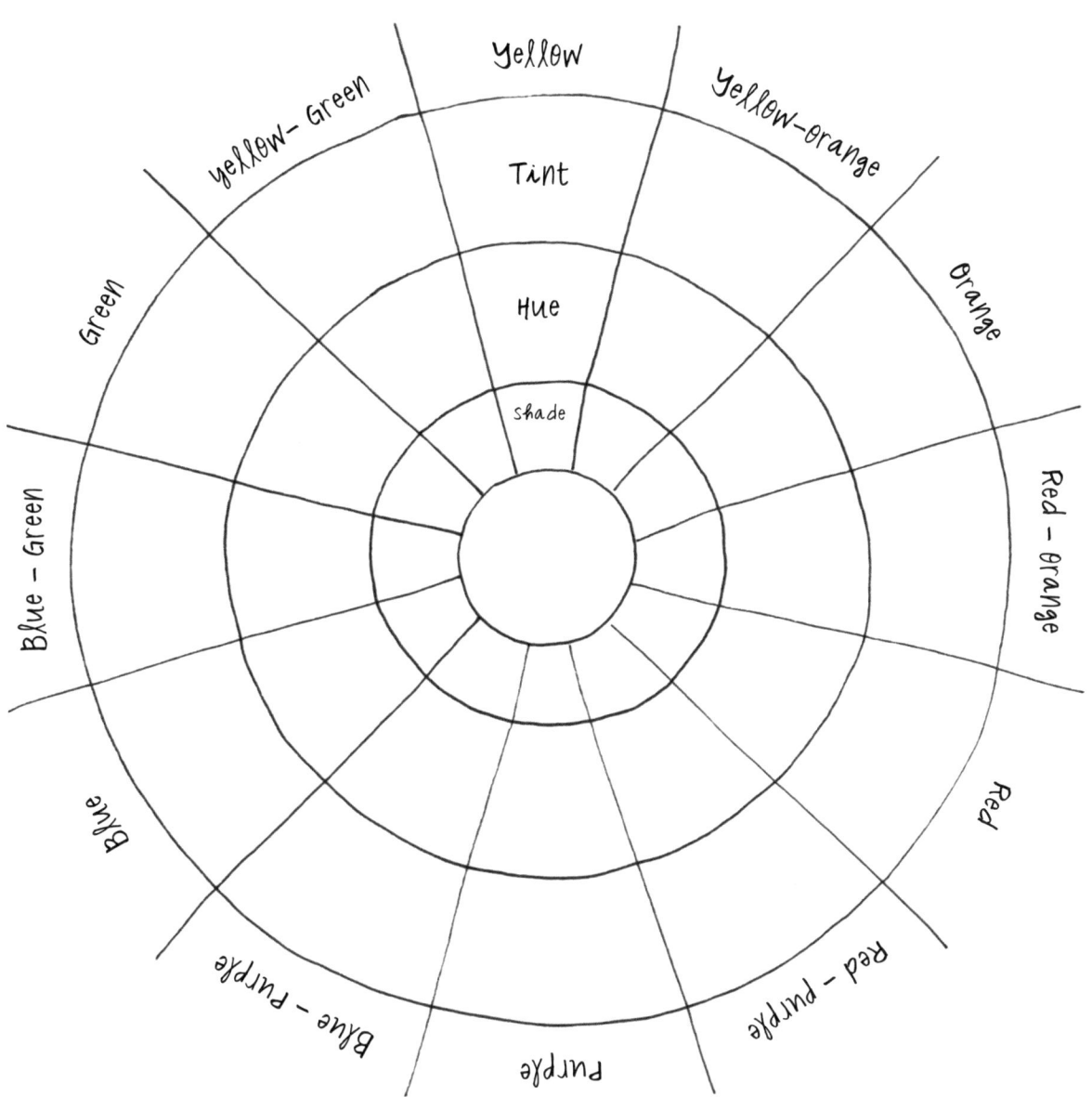

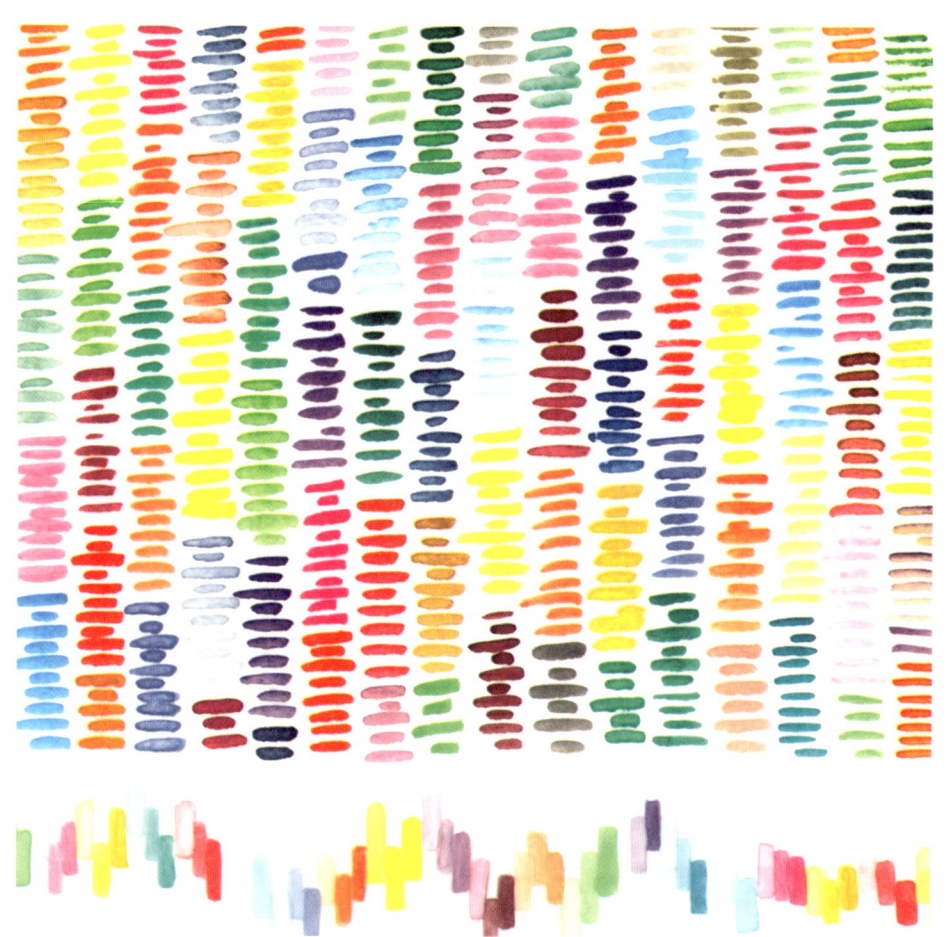

Color Meditation | **LINES**

Think for a second about lines. They can go only horizontal, vertical, or diagonal, or they can go in every direction on the page. They can be thick or thin, they can be watery and drippy, they can start out dark and get light. You can make lines right next to one another or you can give them some space. You can make them along a shape, such as a circle or a triangle, or you can randomly place them all over the page.

▸ Paint some lines

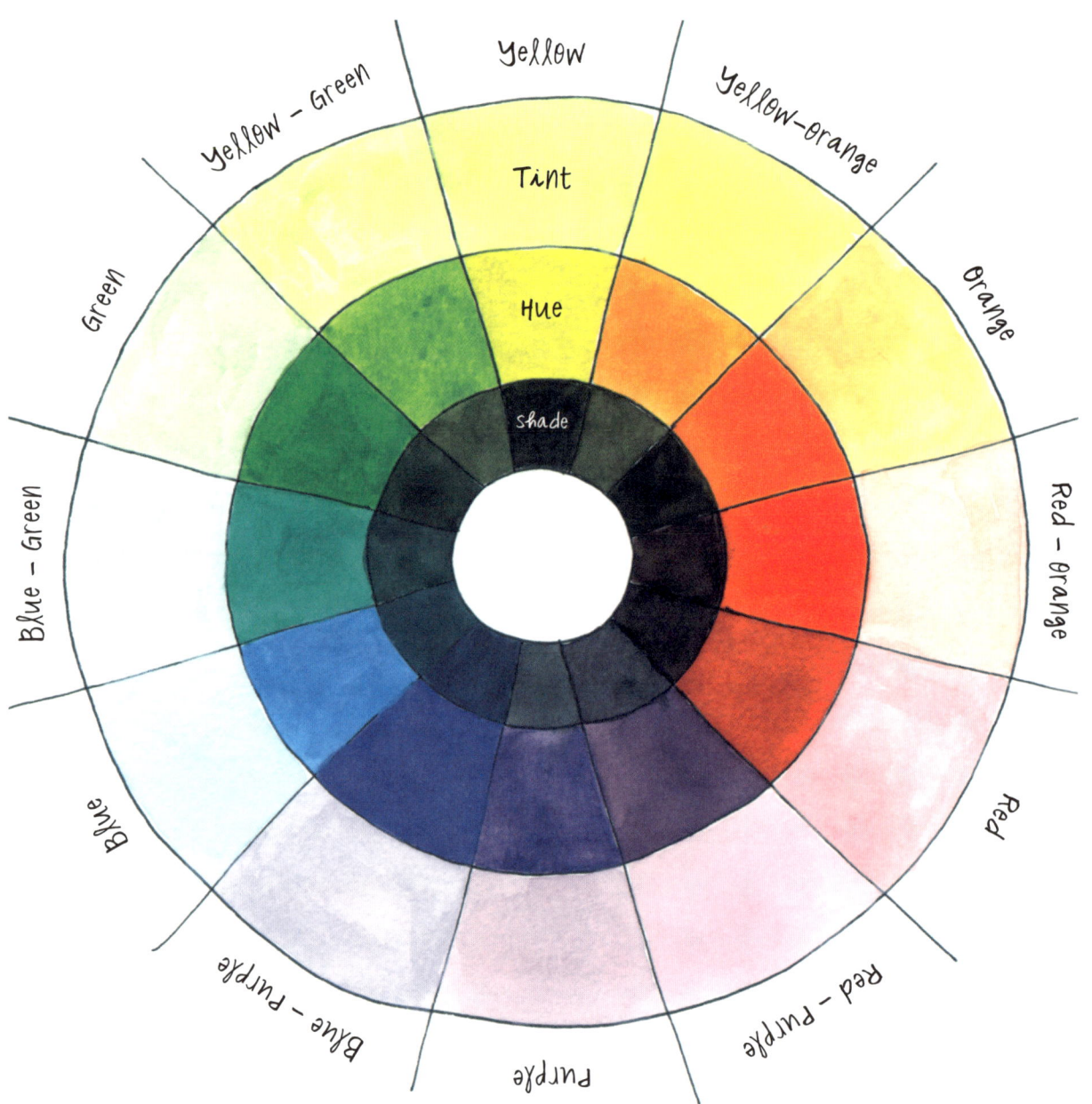

2. MAKE A PERSONAL COLOR WHEEL WITH TINTS AND SHADES

What the heck is a personal color wheel? Well, I don't know about you but I've gotten into some big arguments with folks over the naming of a color. (My dad, in particular. How many sunsets has he claimed were orange that I thought were more pink?) In some cases, you might be able to get a room full of people to agree on a color—if I said "Facebook blue," the room might have a similar color in mind, but if I just said "pear green," everyone would most likely have a different color in their mind. For this color wheel, we're ditching the scientific approach and listening to our guts.

Where the color wheel calls for red, put down your all-time favorite red. If it comes out of the tube, great. If you have to mix colors to get it, great. If you have to mix colors you didn't think would help make a good red but in the end did—like maybe the smallest touch of blue or green—great. Don't take that red to make your favorite orange—although by all means try that because it *might* be your favorite orange—rather, just find or make your favorite orange and put it down.

Stay scientific with your *tints* and *shades*. The dollops of white and black should remain consistent all the way around, but otherwise just have fun.

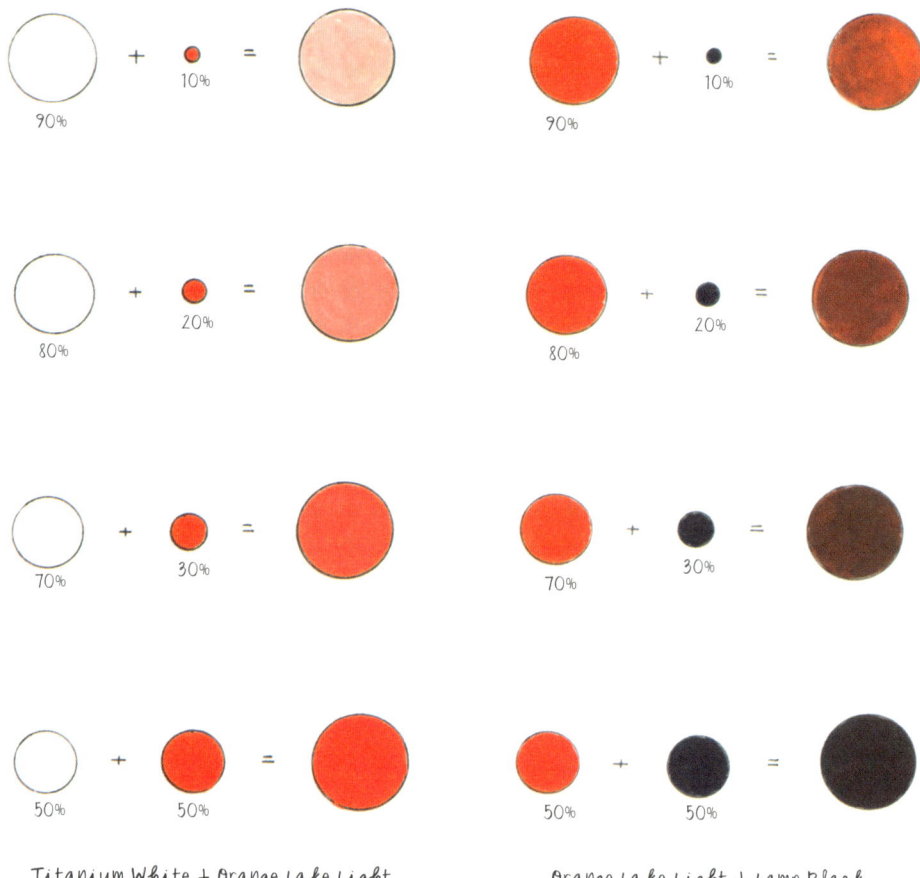

Titanium White + Orange Lake Light   Orange Lake Light + Lamp Black

And what is a personal color wheel good for, you ask? I think it's incredibly helpful to see how all your favorite ideas of color live together. Most likely there's a similarity. In classes when I've had students do this, there's the bright vibrant one, the muted one, the one that leans cool, the one that leans warm. Usually there's a really lovely harmony to the whole thing. And while the complements may not function the way they would on a traditional color wheel, I can almost guarantee they'll still work in a way you'll find useful.

Wasn't that fun? I make a personal color wheel from time to time because my favorite of each hue might change with the seasons or my mood. I'm not a huge fan of royal purples (except in nature)—the purple I gravitate toward can be either magenta or lavender toned—so I often make a personal color wheel starting with purple. It seems to set the tone: if I use a more magenta purple, the other colors lean more jeweled; if I use lavender, the other colors lean brighter and/or more pastel. Making a personal color wheel helps develop your own sense of color harmony—the way that colors work together that is unique to *you*.

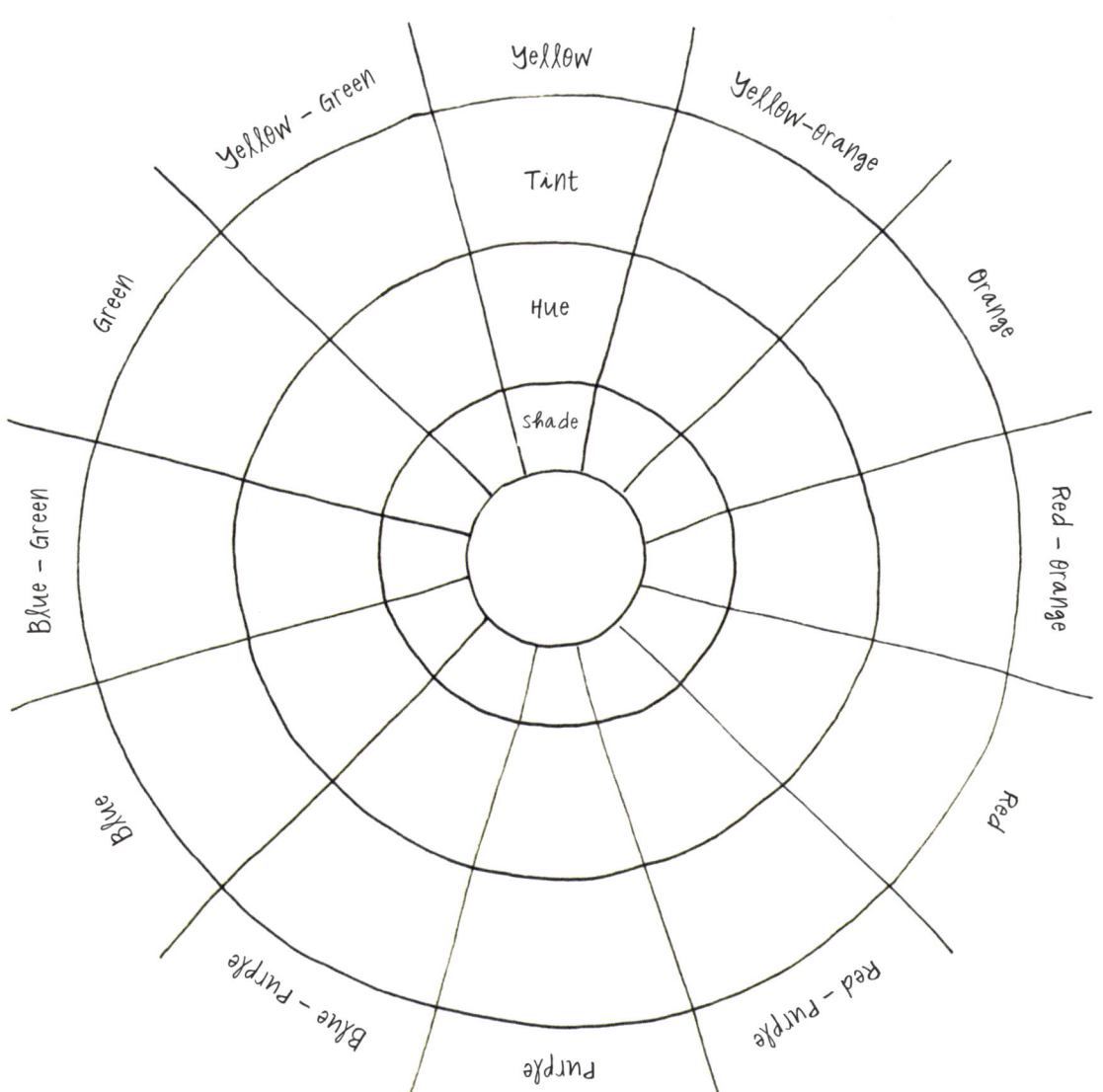

Here's some space to practice making tints and shades. Use any hue you want.

Make some tints. Use the first circle as your guide for white and the second circle for the ratio of your chosen hue. Paint the result in the third circle after the equal sign.

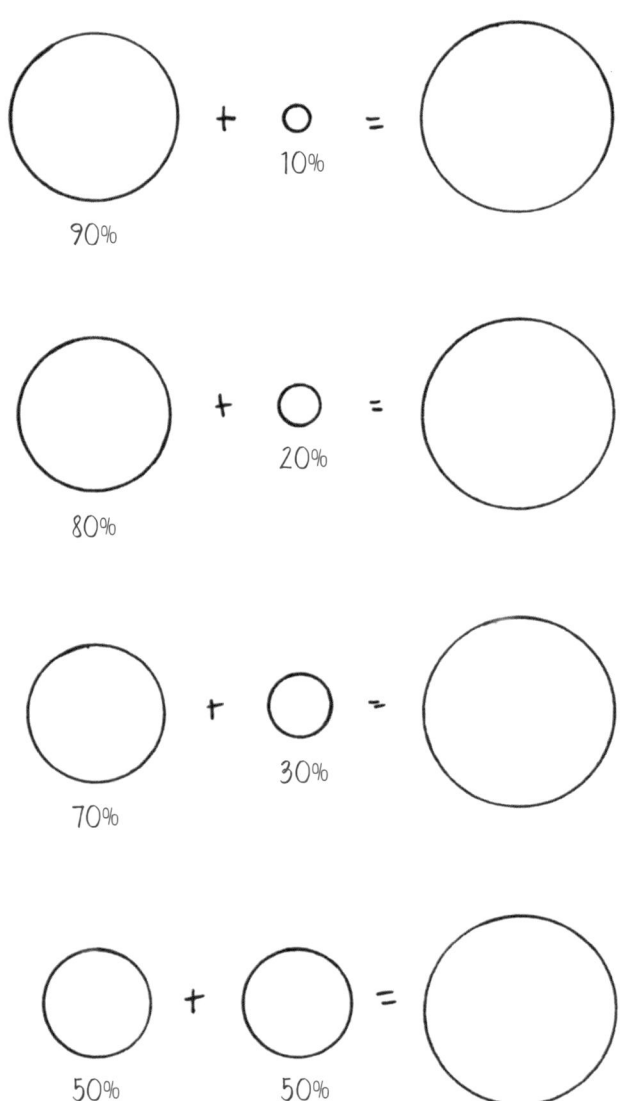

90%   +   10%   =

80%   +   20%   =

70%   +   30%   =

50%   +   50%   =

Make some shades. Use the first circle as your guide for your chosen hue and the second for the ratio of black. Paint the result in the third circle after the equal sign.

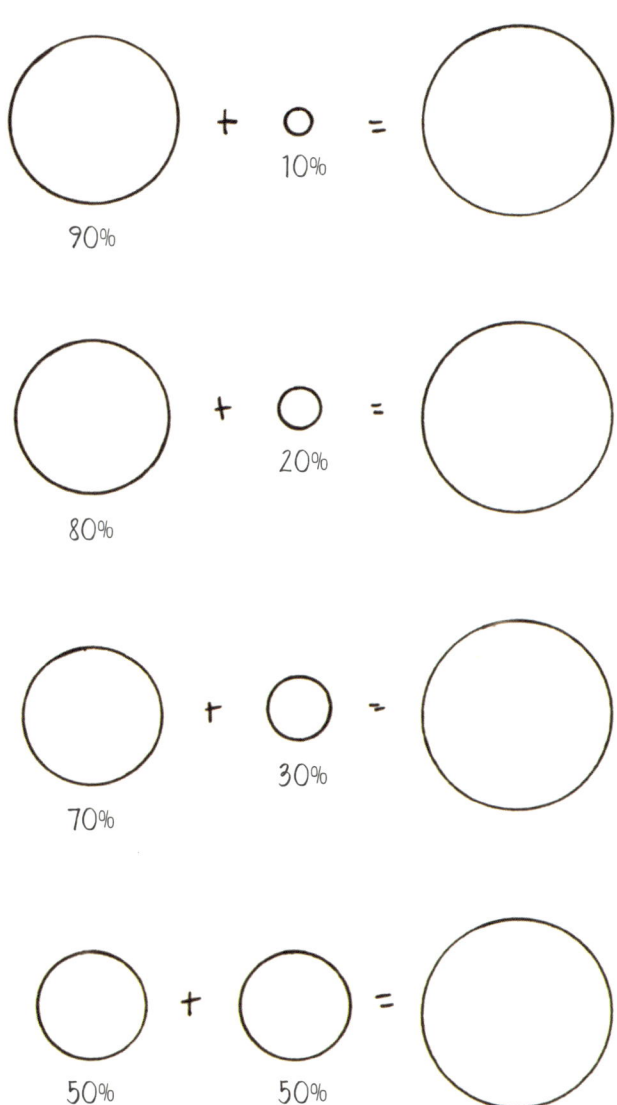

90% + 10% =

80% + 20% =

70% + 30% =

50% + 50% =

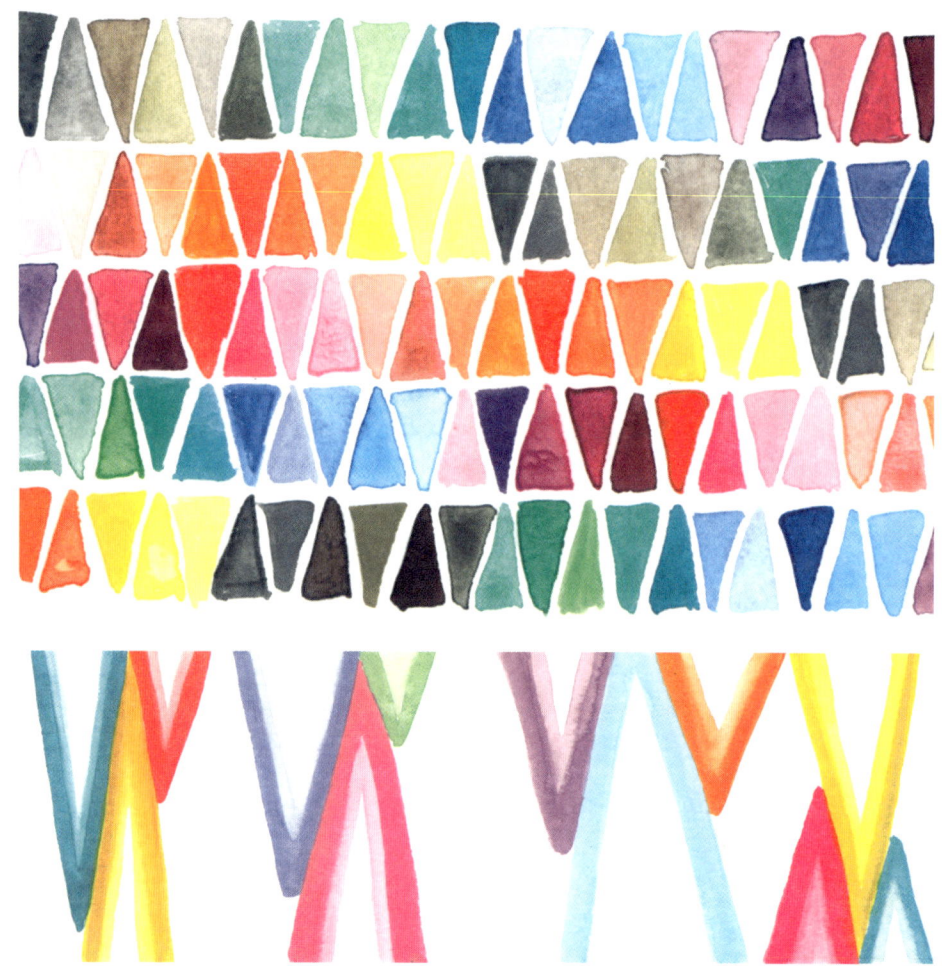

Color Meditation | **TRIANGLES**

Do you remember all the types of triangles? Equilateral: all the sides are equal. Isosceles: two equal sides, two equal angles. Scalene: no congruent sides. You get the idea. Just focus on triangles for a minute. Do you want them to intersect? Be tall and skinny? Short and stubby? Do you want them in neat rows? Point-to-point, back-to-back, or like a quilt?

▸ Paint some triangles

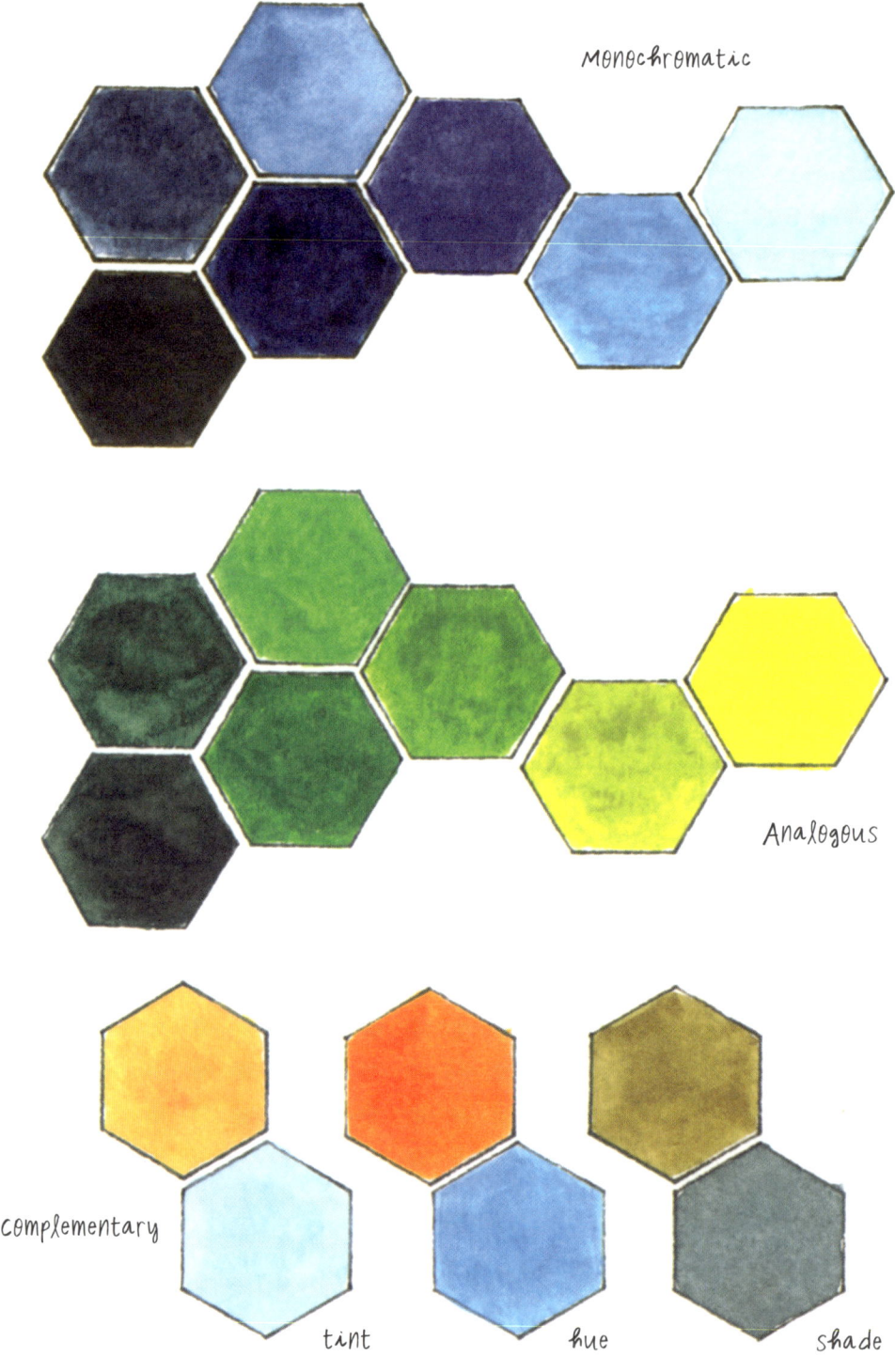

Monochromatic

Analogous

Complementary

tint   hue   shade

3. DIFFERENT COLOR SCHEMES

There are some basic color schemes that are useful to know about. These color schemes can help you understand *color harmony*—when the arrangement of colors is pleasing. Keep in mind that this is super subjective, as one person's harmony is another person's yawn or headache. Regardless, understanding common color schemes will give you some options—especially when you're feeling stuck and not sure what colors to use. Try these!

Use each of these color schemes to fill in the hexagons on the following pages. Once you have a feel for them, pick one color scheme to fill in the illustration that follows. Flip back to your color wheels for reference here as you need to.

Monochromatic. Use one single hue and vary the tints, shades, and saturation. You can also mix your main hue with other ones—just make sure that it still reads within the family of the main hue.

Analogous. These are colors that are next to one another on the color wheel: red, orange, yellow; yellow, green, blue; yellow-green, yellow, yellow-orange. You get the drift. Try this scheme with different tints, shades, and saturations as well. Analogous color schemes are thought to be very harmonic and pleasing to the eye. Sometimes people find it helpful to pick one color as the dominant one and use the other one or two as supporting players.

Complementary. These are colors that are across from one another on the color wheel. The major complements are red/green, blue/orange, purple/yellow. But as you develop more steps on your color wheel, complements expand. So yellow-green's complement is red-purple, or blue-green's complement is red-orange. Complementary colors are generally considered to be on the jarring side of things. They grab your attention. They tend to make a statement. Because of this they're used constantly in advertising and sports. (Once you know this you'll never be able to unsee it.) Try using complements with different tints, shades, and saturations as well.

Triatic. Here's where we get into lesser used but still interesting schemes. This one, as the name implies, is centered around a triangle. So colors that are equally spaced on a color wheel, e.g., yellow, red, blue (or the primaries!); yellow-orange, purple, green; green-yellow, red-orange, blue-purple... This scheme can be a bit tricky, but it definitely works. (Look around for things that employ them; there's a lot of design that utilizes primary colors—go find it!) And here, again I'll suggest you remember to try tints, shades, and different saturations of your colors.

Split-Complementary. This scheme also uses three colors but a bit differently. Instead of just using the direct complement, you use the two surrounding colors on the color wheel. Most people think this scheme is a bit less visually intense than a direct complementary scheme. Examples: green, red-orange, red-purple; yellow, red-purple, blue-purple; blue-green, orange, red.

Random. For fun, let's throw in a dice-determined, more random option. You'll see here six numbers, each assigned a color. Roll a die or use a random number generator to choose a color step-by-step. If you roll a one, which calls for red, pick any red that suits your fancy. Keep rolling the die for each area you need to fill. If you get red twice you can use the same red or make a different one.

Triatic

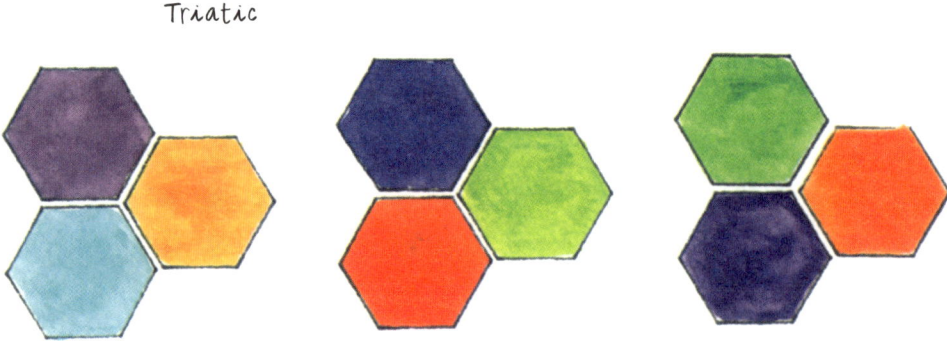

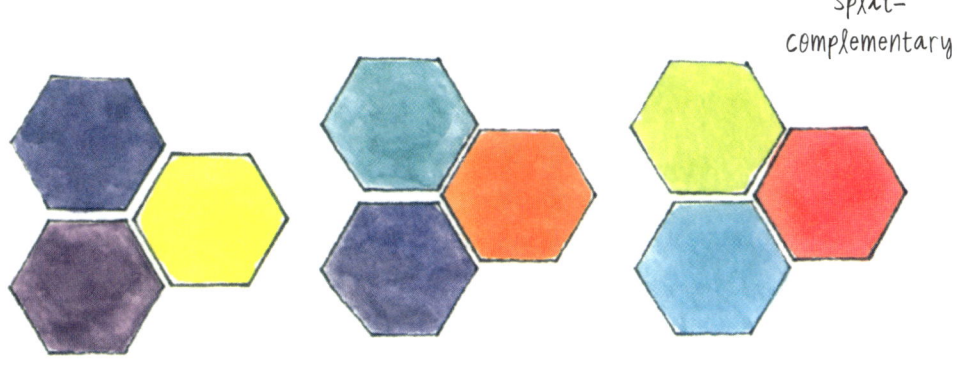

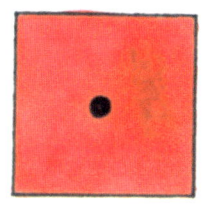 one = red

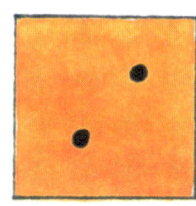 two = orange

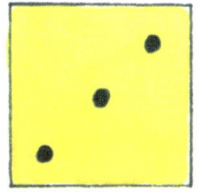 three = yellow

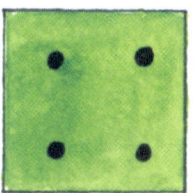 four = green

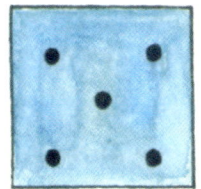 five = blue

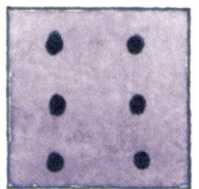 six = purple

Fill in these hexagons with the labeled color scheme in any way you choose!

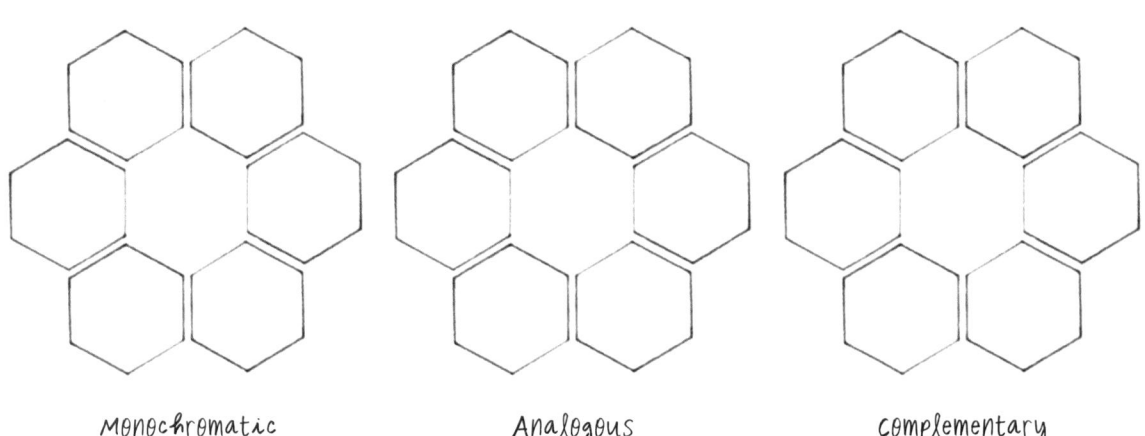

Monochromatic   Analogous   Complementary

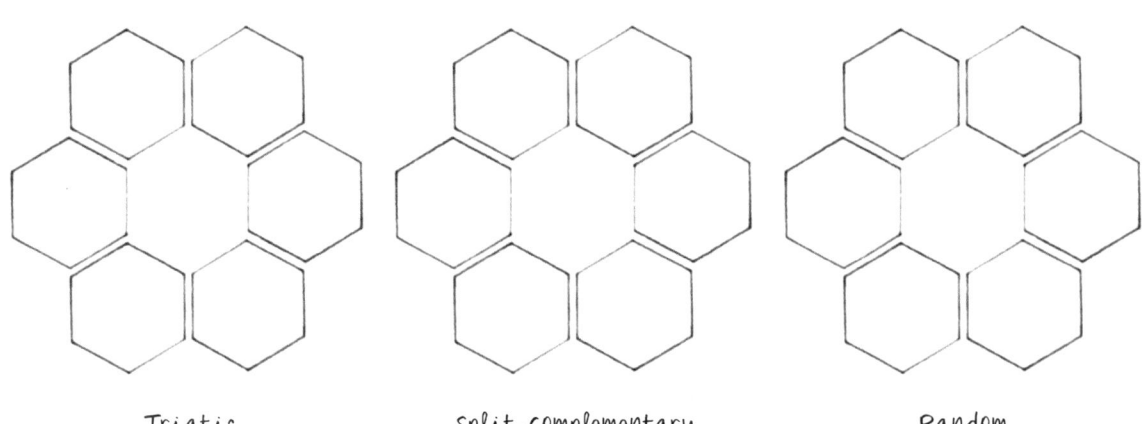

Triatic   Split-complementary   Random

Fill in each illustration with the labeled color scheme. Seeing them side by side should give you a better understanding of how they work. Don't forget to refer to your color wheels on pages 27 and 33 to help you fill out these color schemes.

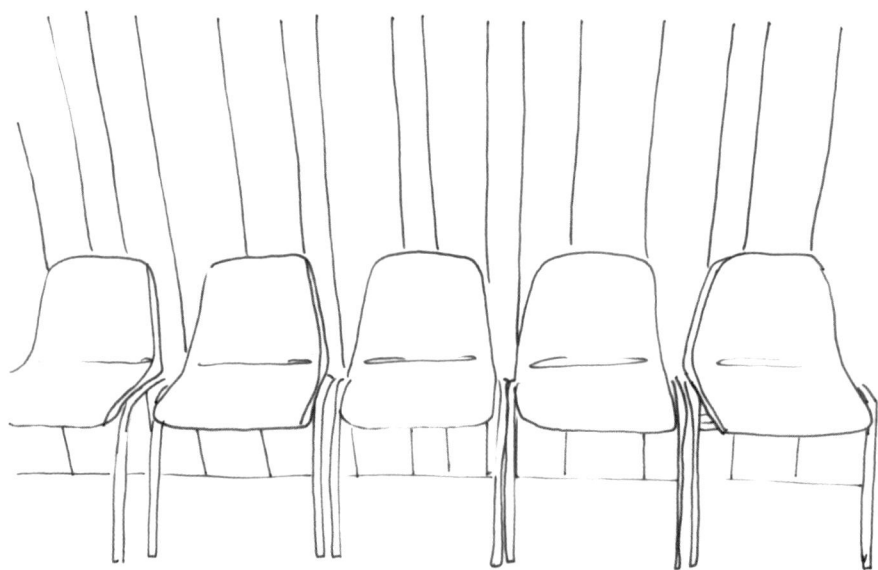

Monochromatic

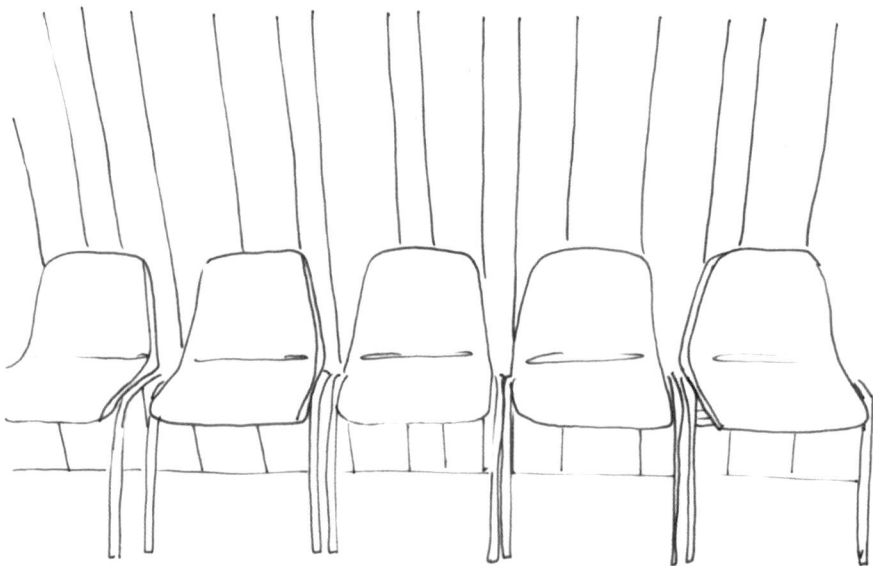

Analogous

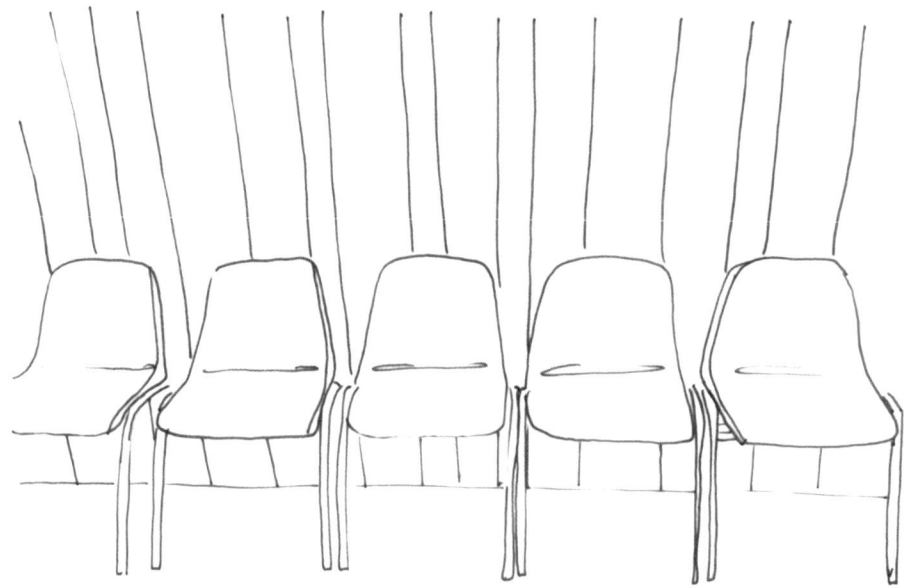

complementary

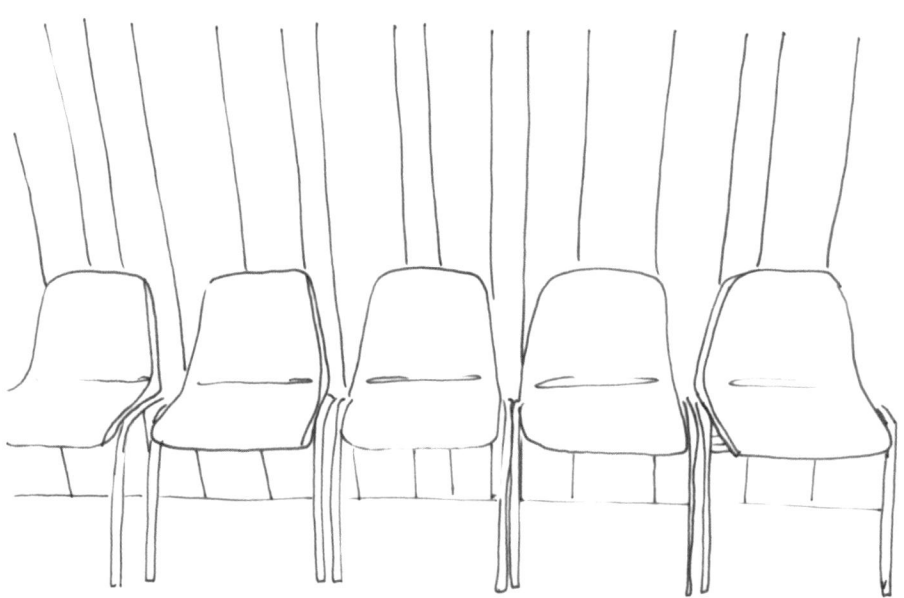

Triatic

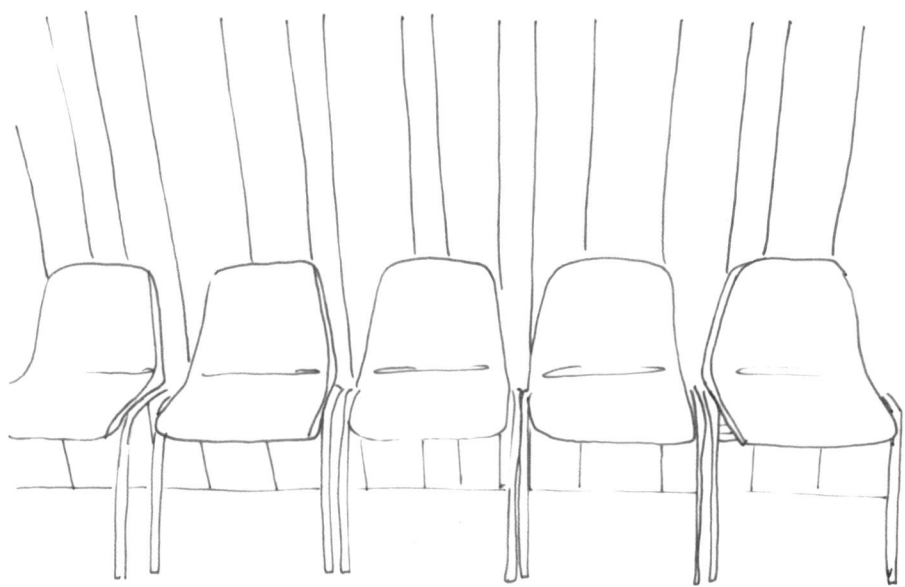

split-complementary

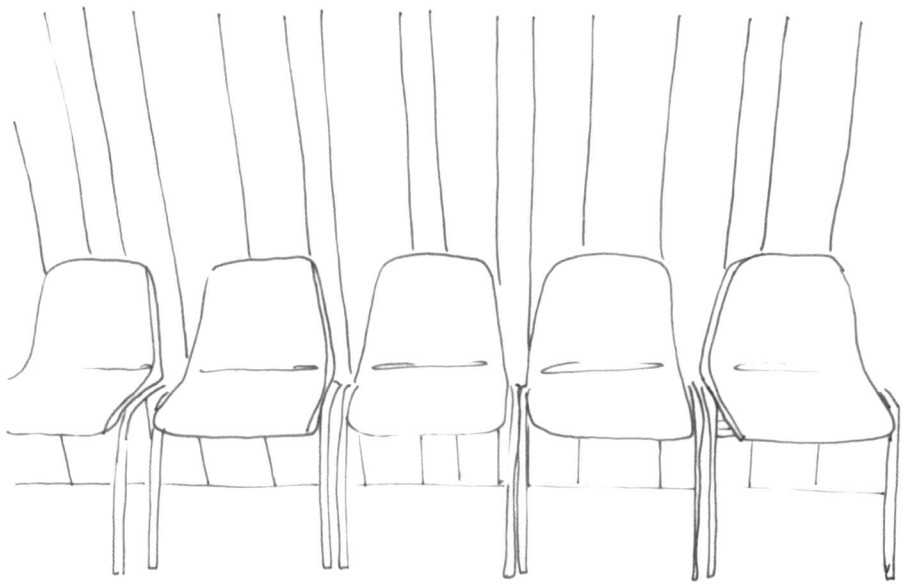

Random

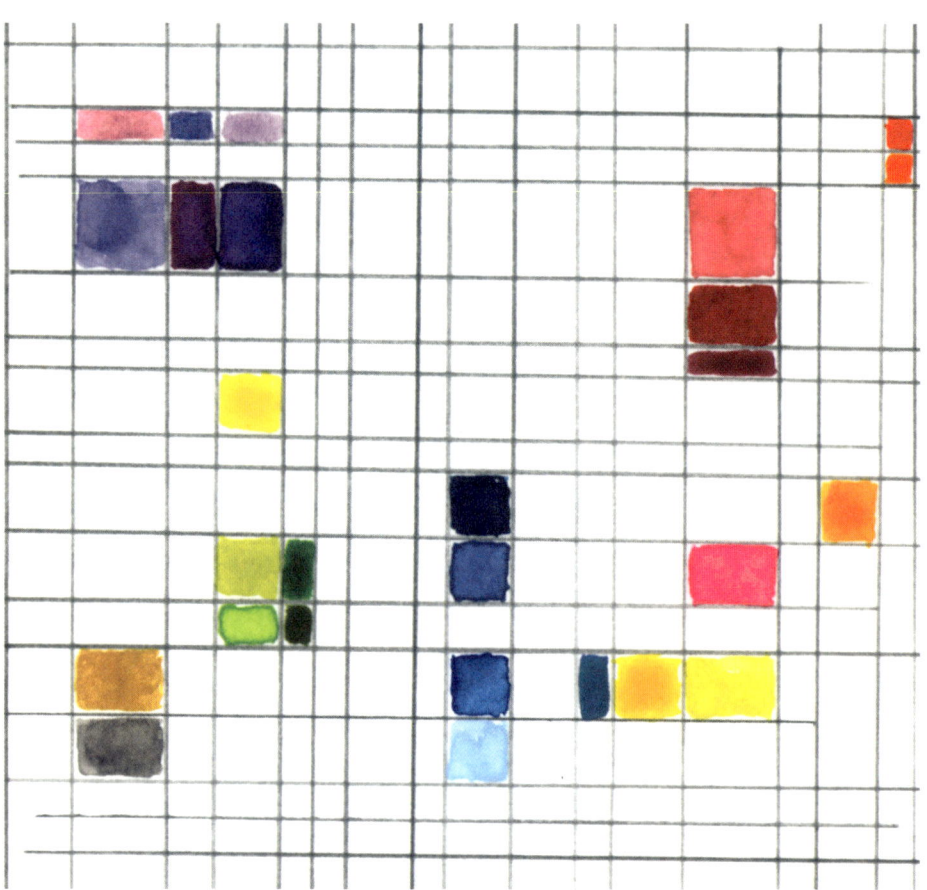

Color Meditation | **SQUARES**

Oh, the square. I happen to be a fan. I love grids (especially gridded paper). I love square compositions and gravitate to them in my own work. Do you want to draw a grid and fill it in square by square with different colors? (Your grid can even be wonky. I promise I won't be the square police and call you out.) Do you want to stack squares? Make a little chart? Paint a concentric square so it feels like it's getting bigger and bigger? (This might seem like it's more like stripes, but what the heck—break the rules.)

▸ Paint some squares

A watercolor color-mixing chart. Both the top row headers and the left column headers list the following colors in the same order:

Lemon Yellow, Cadmium Yellow, Scarlet Lake, Red Rouge, Rose Opera, Alizeron Crimson, Green Vert, Olive Green, Cerulean Blue, French Ultramarine, Turquoise Light, Cobalt, Yellow Ochre, Raw Sienna, Burnt Sienna, Indian Red, Burnt Umber, Dioxide Violet, Paynes Gray, Neutral Gray, Lamp Black, Chinese White

4. CHARTING YOUR PAINT BOX

I love charts. I love looking at them. I love making them. I love devising new ways of using them. When I buy any new supplies—from paints to colored pencils, I like to make a chart of what the colors look like. I love writing the names of the colors down. It just makes me happy. *But*, charting paint colors in two directions is super useful, especially in wet media. If you make a cross-reference chart, you can see how your colors are going to interact.

To make a chart of your paint colors, dedicate one vertical line and one horizontal line for each color. (In the chart I made, I included twenty-two of my colors.) Label each color, then carefully paint the colors row by row. Wait for each row to dry before you paint the vertical columns. Because watercolor and even gouache—if you add enough water—are transparent you'll quickly see how the colors interact. I refer to my chart when I'm thinking about mixing or layering colors. Do I want a redder brown or a grayer brown? The chart helps me determine which color will get me where I want to go.

▶ Paint your own chart

If you'd prefer, you can make a color chart by mixing your colors separately instead of painting stripes. I actually like to do both, and you can see how each has a slightly different result. Just remember to label your colors, follow the chart, and keep your brush clean between each mixing round so you get clear results.

Kuretake Watercolors	no. 31	no. 33	no. 40	no. 42	no. 51	no. 55	no. 50	no. 61	no. 62	no. 38
no. 31										
no. 33										
no. 40										
no. 42										
no. 51										
no. 55										
no. 50										
no. 61										
no. 62										
no. 38										

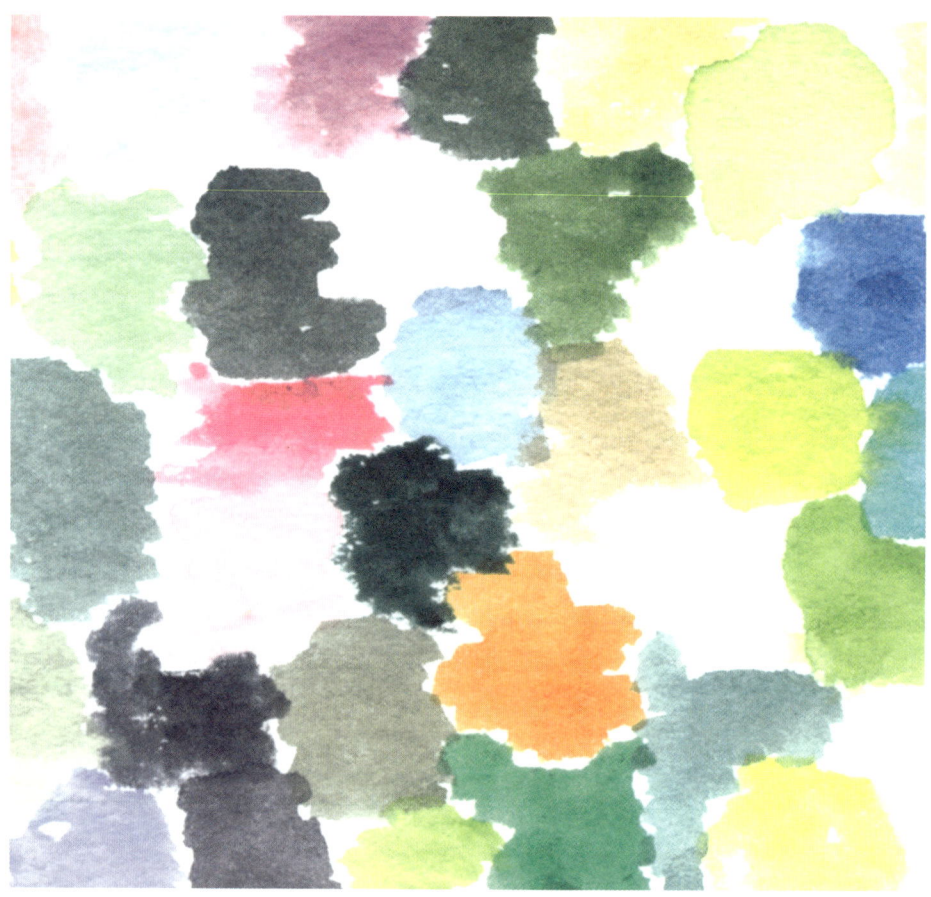

Color Meditation | **ABSTRACT SHAPES**

What is abstraction? It can mean taking something familiar and altering it so it's not quite as recognizable. It can mean not being inspired by anything in particular and just making some marks. As I mentioned before, I prefer to repeat the same shape in my color meditations because I love how that looks on the page, but feel free to go nuts here and just make a bunch of different abstract shapes. Maybe you have a brush that makes a really cool mark if you wiggle it while you paint. Maybe you want to splatter a little bit.

▸ Paint some abstract shapes

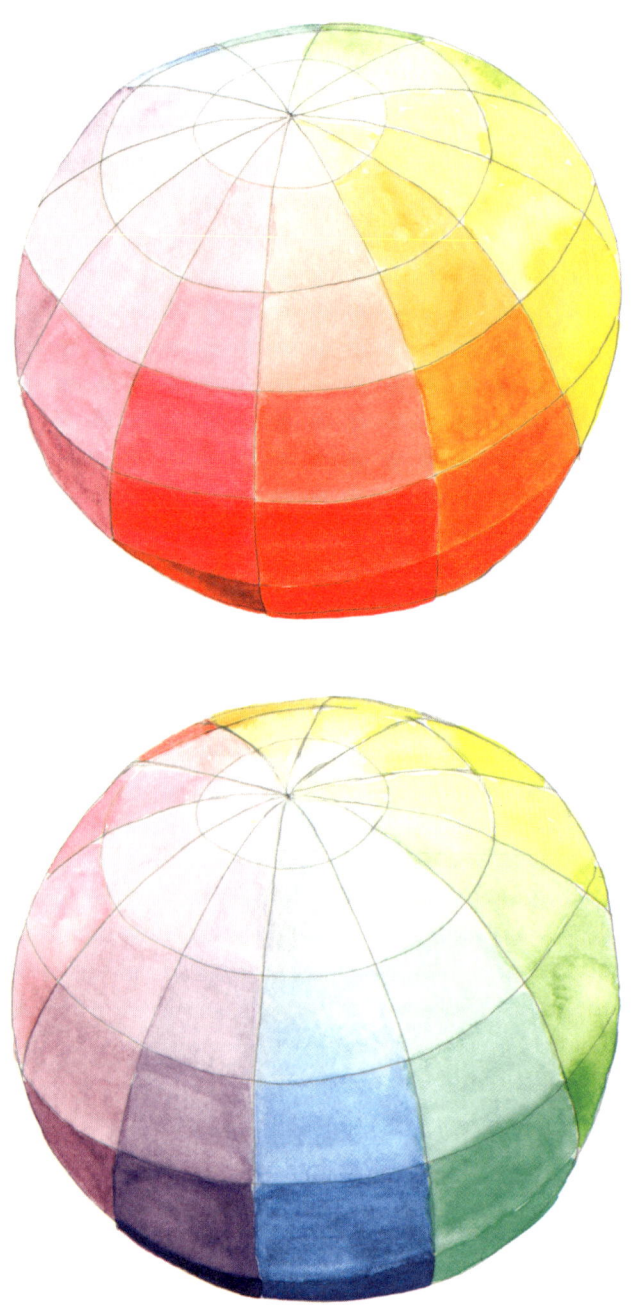

This is my take on a "saturation globe," inspired by Philipp Otto Runge.

5. | SATURATION

Let's work on the concept of saturation. With water-based media, we play with saturation by adding water. Below you'll see a ten-step saturation scale. Pick a single color and add it at full strength (which is the color with the least amount of water in it to make it move and be paintable) to a palette or a little container. Make sure you have enough to paint in your first square plus some extra. You'll need enough of this base paint to tackle the entire scale. I'd say that enough to fill three to four squares at full strength should be a good starting point. My favorite way to complete a saturation scale is to literally add drops of water to the palette container while you paint out each square. I use a dropper and a small vial of clean water to do this. This way it feels (and is) more scientific.

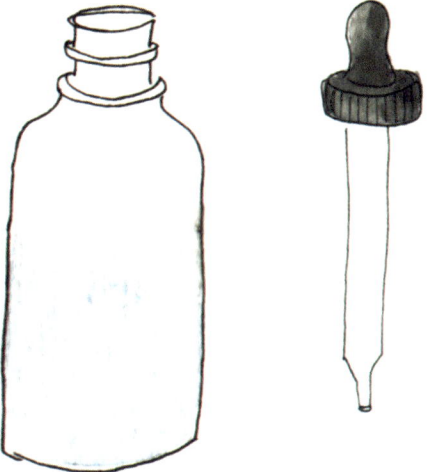

After you paint your first square at full strength, put two to three drops of water into your color and paint square number two. Repeat and repeat until you get to the final square. Be sure to fully immerse and swish your brush into each more desaturated version of your color or this won't work. The brush will retain the last strength, and if you just dip, it won't get light enough quick enough. You can also blot and clean your brush between each saturation stage if you aren't seeing the color desaturate fast enough. You might need to do this exercise more than once to get it right. Don't sweat that.

Once you fill in all the squares, paint the same color out in a saturation scale with just a brush. For this you'll need just a little bit of the color at full strength, clean water, and a paper towel or blotting cloth. Make your initial mark. Blot the brush on your towel and dip it gently into the water, go over the right edge of your mark and spread the color out (it should look lighter). Blot the brush again, dip again (don't overdip or really swish; you just need a little water), go over the right edge and keep spreading the color out. Continue until the paint looks like barely tinted water.

Gaining control of saturation can help you with all sorts of other things in painting, such as making a gradient sky or a reflection of light. It also can help when you're layering colors—you can make a darker or lighter purple or green by changing the saturation of blue or yellow and painting over your initial hue. A purple with a blue desaturated wash on it will look different than that purple with a yellow desaturated wash.

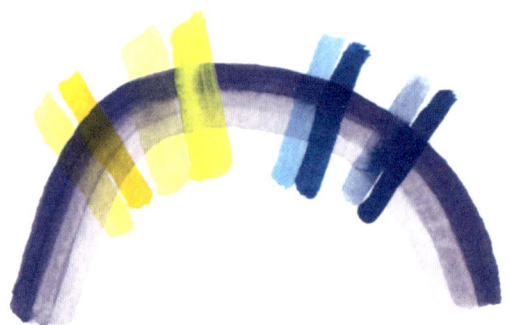

Practice a saturation scale here.

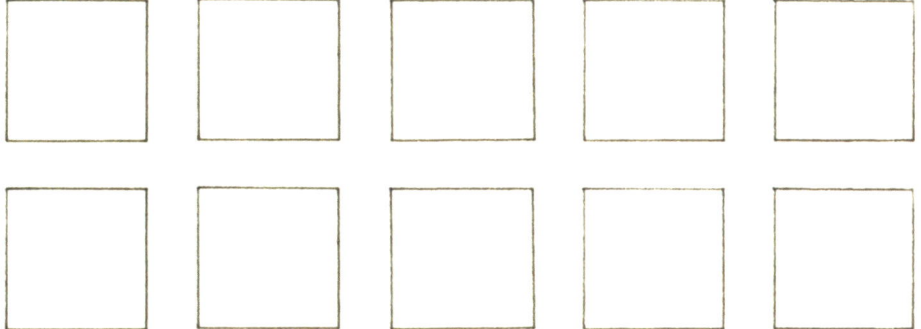

Practice painting out a saturation scale here.

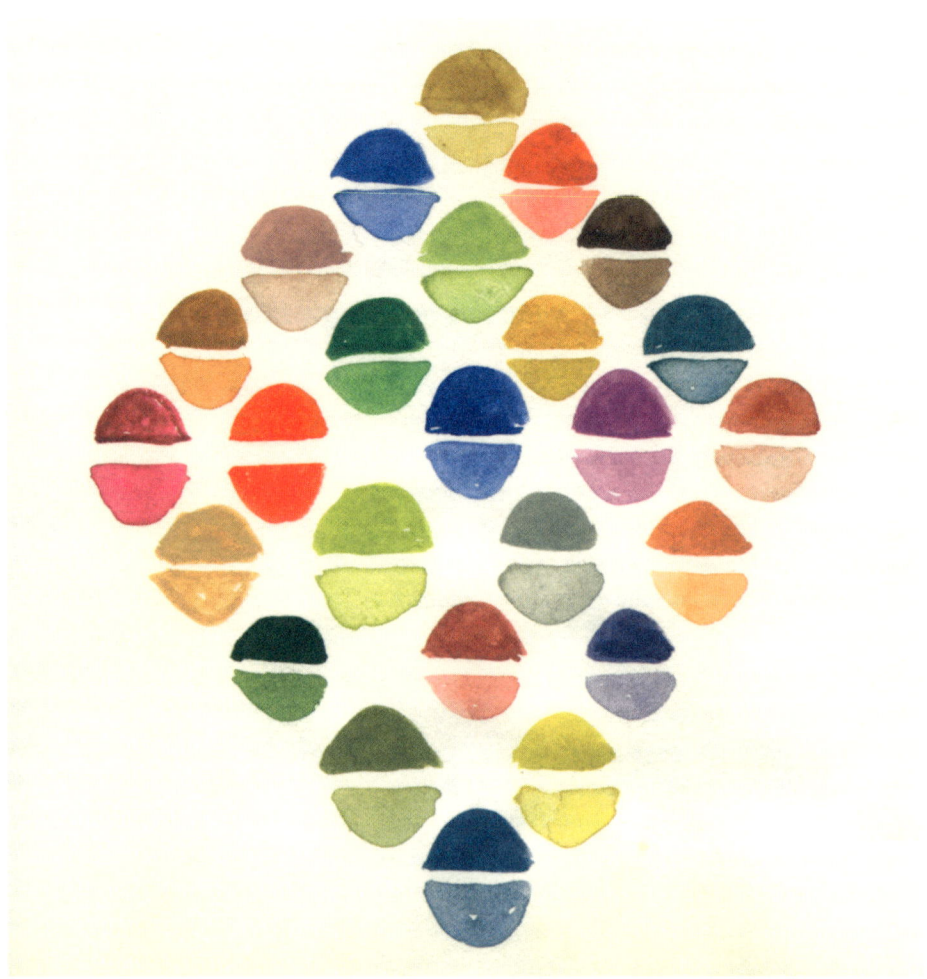

Color Meditation | **HALF CIRCLES**

What's got more potential than a dot or a circle, you ask? I just might say a half circle. You can place them so they almost make a whole circle. That lovely little bit of negative space between them is pretty great, right? You can create a line of them facing only one direction. You can create a pattern with varying sizes and directions of half circles all over the page.

▸ Paint some half circles

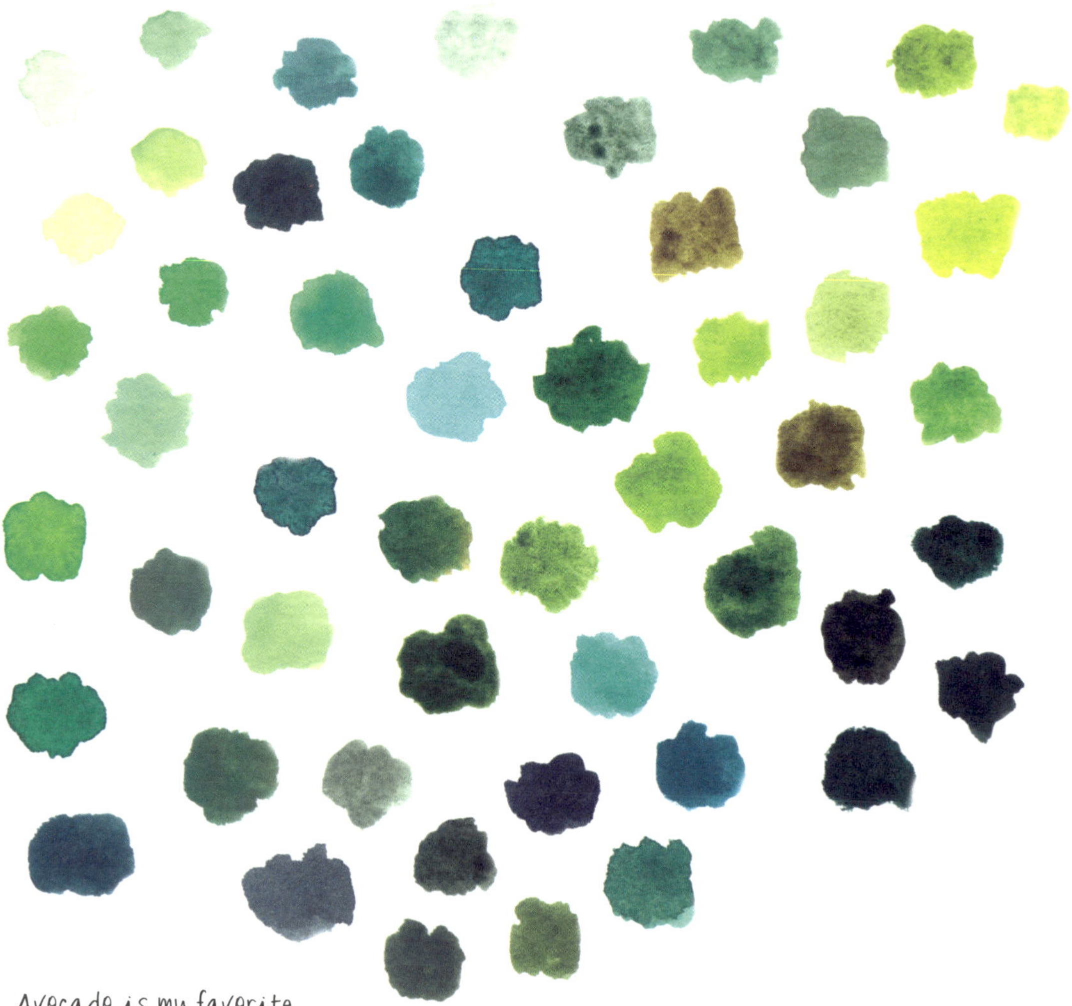

Avocado is my favorite
shade of green.

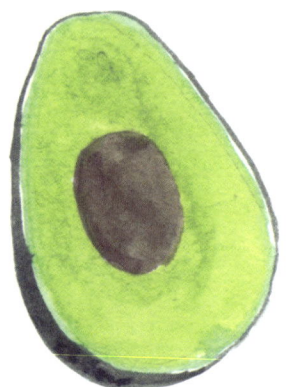

Notes: Yellow + green makes me
very happy (lemon grass!)
Also good when white added
(limeade!)
When does green become turquoise?
Not a fan of green green (viridian)
except in nature

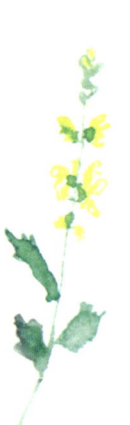

One of the most important things to learn about color and color mixing is that often the *tiniest* amount of another color will generate an immense shift or alteration in your original hue. You might also be surprised—sometimes adding what you think might be the wrong color actually makes the perfect color. Oftentimes adding a small amount of a complementary color—say, a tiny bit of bright green to a bright red—will result in a richer and truer color than you'd imagine.

This exercise is meant to free you up. You're going to pick an original hue—preferably one that comes straight from a tube—and try adding any and all colors to this original in varying amounts. Go for the obvious—add black and white—but try to see how crazy you can get too! In fact, try mixing some colors together first, such as a yellow and orange to make a tangerine, before you add it to your original. Try adding in different increments:

20 percent gray, 80 percent original

20 percent gray, 10 percent yellow, 70 percent original

30 percent gray, 30 percent yellow, 40 percent original

As you mix, try to make sure that your new color still reads as part of your original family. For example, if your original was blue and you add red, don't add so much red as to make a purple; make sure it still reads mostly as a blue, although a purplish one. Put down small swatches of each color as you go. You get the idea, right?

Your goal is to make twenty or thirty—or why not try fifty?!?—different colors. The more the merrier, right? Obviously you can do this exercise over and over and over with multiple original colors.

For fun, *name* all your colors. Of course, you don't *need* to do this, but I sort of love it. I secretly wanted to grow up to be the person who named all the lipstick colors. Honestly, though, naming things helps you place and understand them. Also, it expands your color-naming ability in life. (The color geek in me loves calling a green viridian, pistachio, or emerald, rather than just green.)

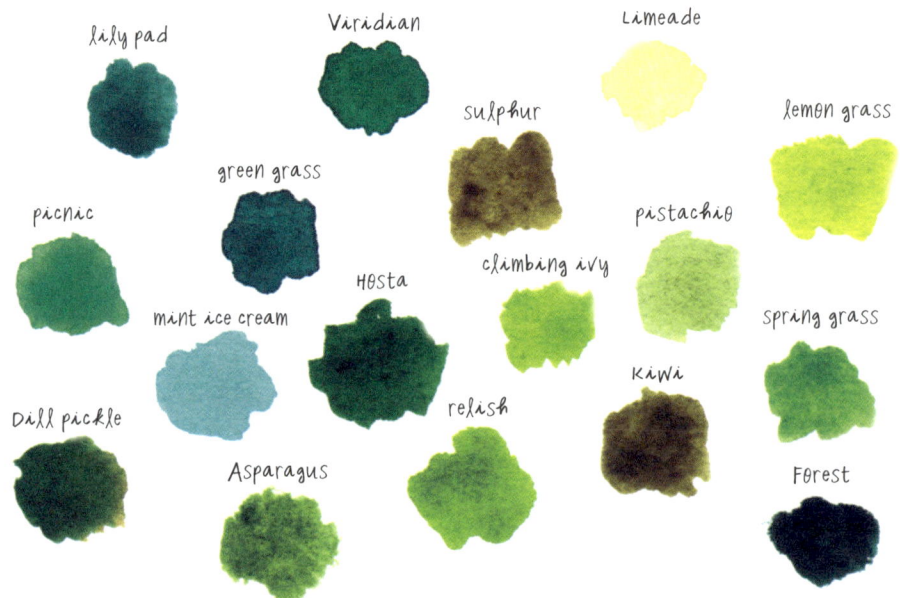

lily pad
Viridian
Limeade
sulphur
lemon grass
green grass
pistachio
picnic
climbing ivy
Hosta
spring grass
mint ice cream
Kiwi
Dill pickle
relish
Asparagus
Forest

PRO TIP: As you make these colors, you might fall in love with one. (Oh, I hope you do!) Try to write down the formula for it. It doesn't have to be exact, but jot down that you used a tad of cerulean, with a touch of lemon yellow, and, if you can, guess percentages. I do this when I know I need to get back to a color. It helps immensely.

Make as many as you can of one color. Bonus points for naming them and making observations about your thoughts and process.

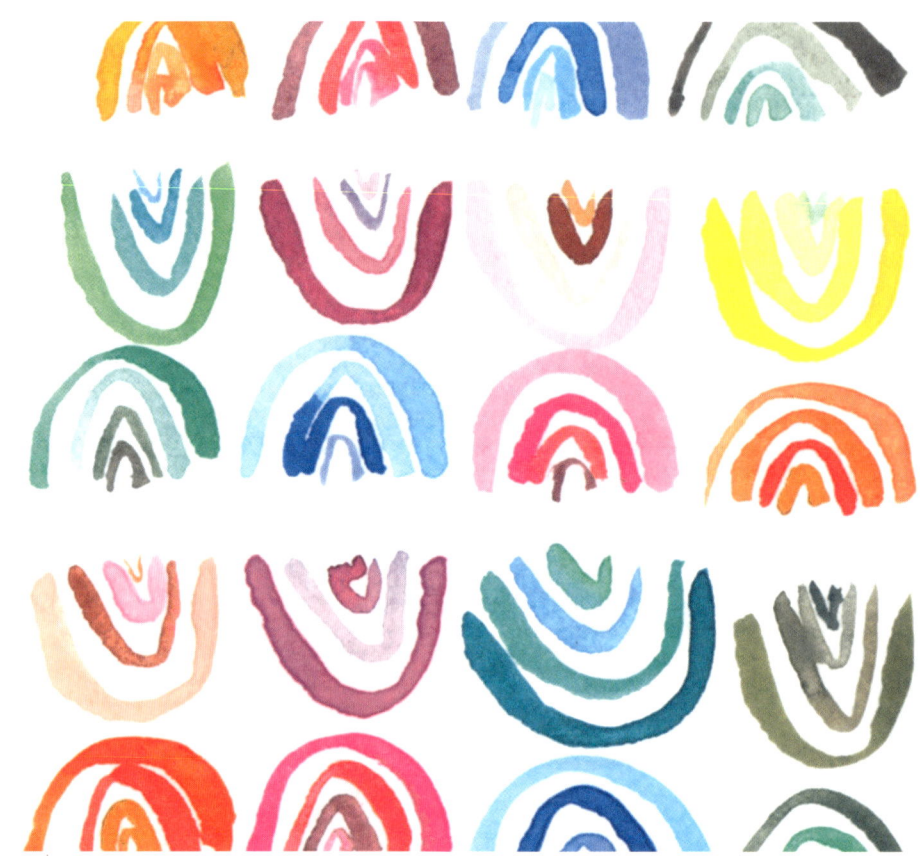

Color Meditation | **RAINBOWS**

"My heart leaps up when I behold a rainbow in the sky." I had to memorize this William Wordsworth poem in high school and it's stuck with me—I do love me a rainbow. What's not to love? But hey, think about the rainbow if it's *not* in rainbow order. Or what if it has three colors instead of seven? What if you want some dreary rainbows? I'm a fan of shifting our internalized relationships to things. Make happy things sad, big things small, scary things funny. What if they're camouflaged in the sky? What if they're upside down— do they look like smiles? What do they look like nested, in rows, in a pattern?

▸ Paint some rainbows

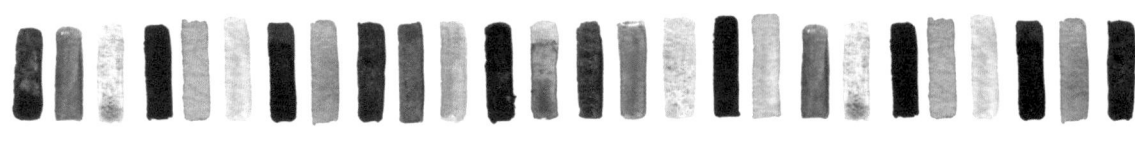

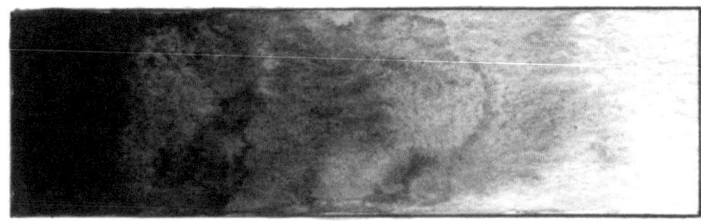

Mars Black

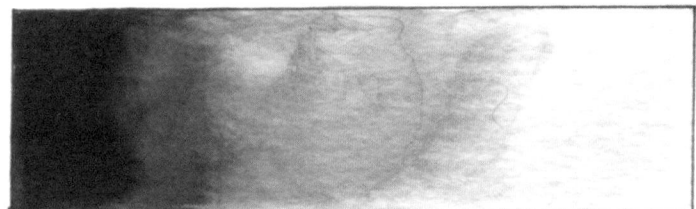

Lamp Black

Ivory Black

7. | FOUR WAYS TO BLACK

Hopefully the color wheel exercise taught you exactly how powerful black can be, but let's talk about black for a second. There are generally two kinds of black that you can get: *ivory* and *mars*. What's the difference, you ask? Good question. While each company may have a slightly different formula for their paints, here's the general difference.

IVORY (aka Bone, Charcoal, Lamp) This black:	MARS This black:
• Is based on *carbon*	• Is based on *iron*
• Tends to have a brownish undertone, although some lamp blacks read a bit blue	• Tends to have a bluer undertone
• Reads warmer	• Reads cooler and is also more neutral; will make a more familiar gray
• Has a moderate strength to alter a color	• Is stronger than ivory black in altering power
• Is usually more transparent in nature	• Is opaque

Take the blacks you have and paint them out (refer back to the saturation exercise if you need a refresher on how to do this) so you can see how they lean toward warm or cool. Also take a pool of a color and add black to it in a percentage. You'll see how a little black goes a long way—and how you can have blacks that reflect a single hue, aka a blue black or a red black (this is useful, say, if you're trying to indicate a certain kind of light that's reflecting even in the darkest parts of your painting).

Here's how these three blacks interact with rose.
This helps clarify how different they are.

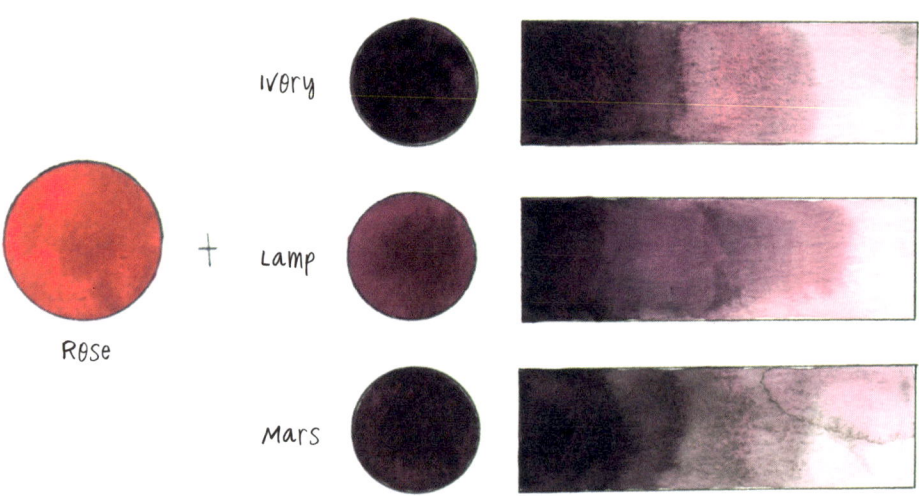

Ivory

Rose   +   Lamp

Mars

PRO TIP: Have I mentioned lately that using colors right out of the tube is one of the biggest giveaways that you're a beginning painter? Also, black is a *powerful* color, right? The smallest amount can change a color immediately. If you're interested in making "naturalistic" paintings I really recommend learning how to make your own black. You can also then push your blacks into a family (e.g., red, yellow, green, blue, brown, etc.) that can enhance the painting you're working on.

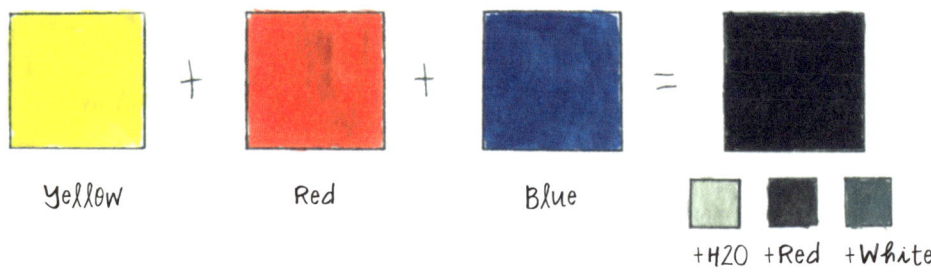

Yellow   +   Red   +   Blue   =

+H2O +Red +White

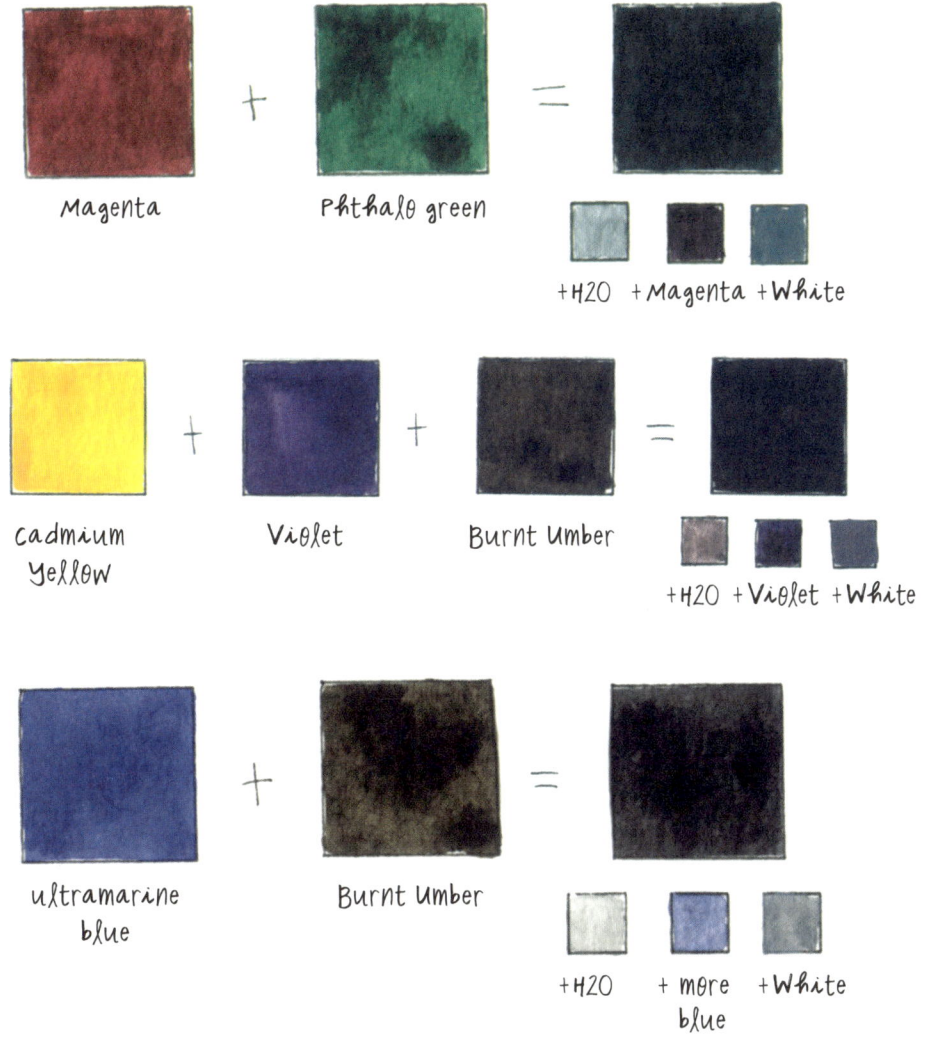

Magenta + Phthalo green =

+H2O +Magenta +White

cadmium Yellow + Violet + Burnt Umber =

+H2O +Violet +White

ultramarine blue + Burnt Umber =

+H2O + more blue +White

What is the easiest basic formula for black? Ultramarine blue + a brown—I find burnt umber is the best for a rich dark black, but any brown will do. Raw sienna will make a lighter, more ruddy black. Burnt sienna is darker than raw sienna, still red leaning, but not as dark as burnt umber black. You get the picture, right? Try to make a whole bunch of different blacks. Then try to push them into other color families. Be sure to paint them out so you can see how transparent they are and observe the underlying color—and then add white to them to see what kind of gray they make.

Now make your own versions of black!

Label these squares with the colors you use to make black. Use the small squares as you experiment, adding water, more of one hue, and white to your black.

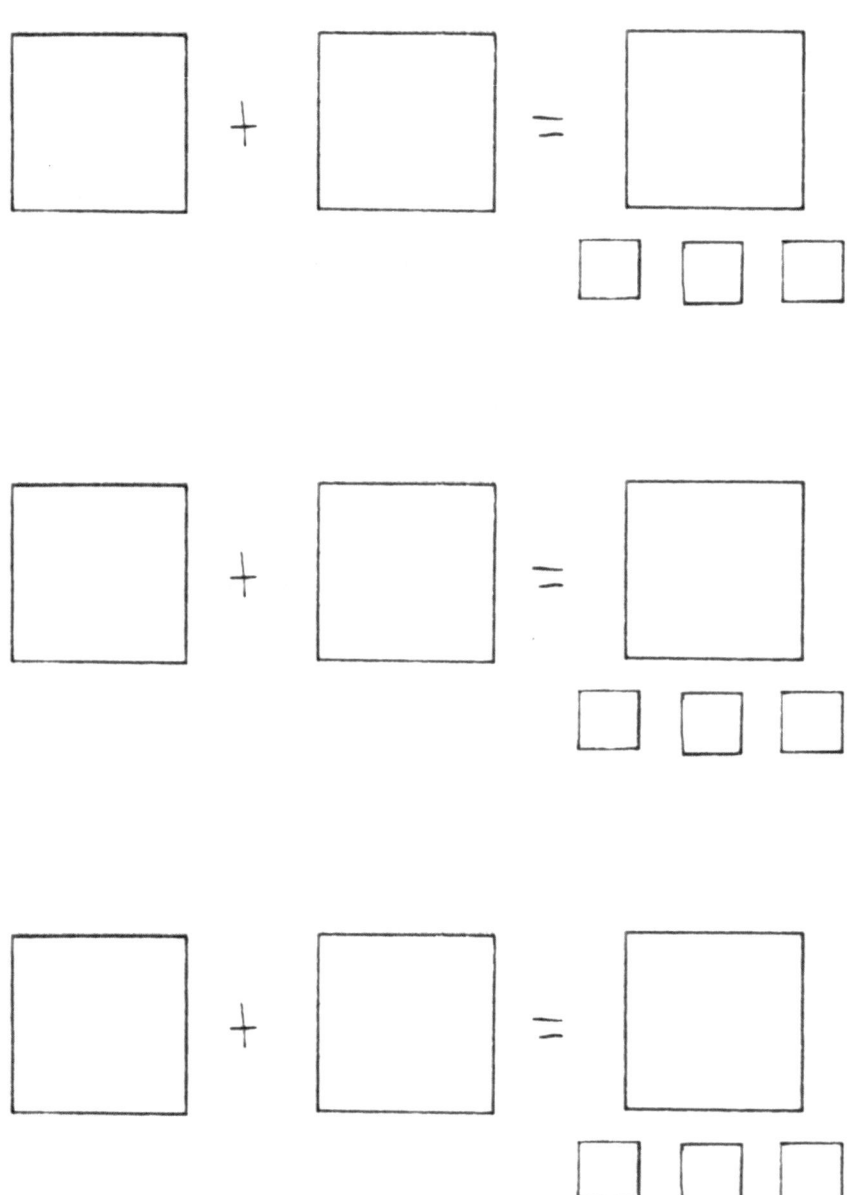

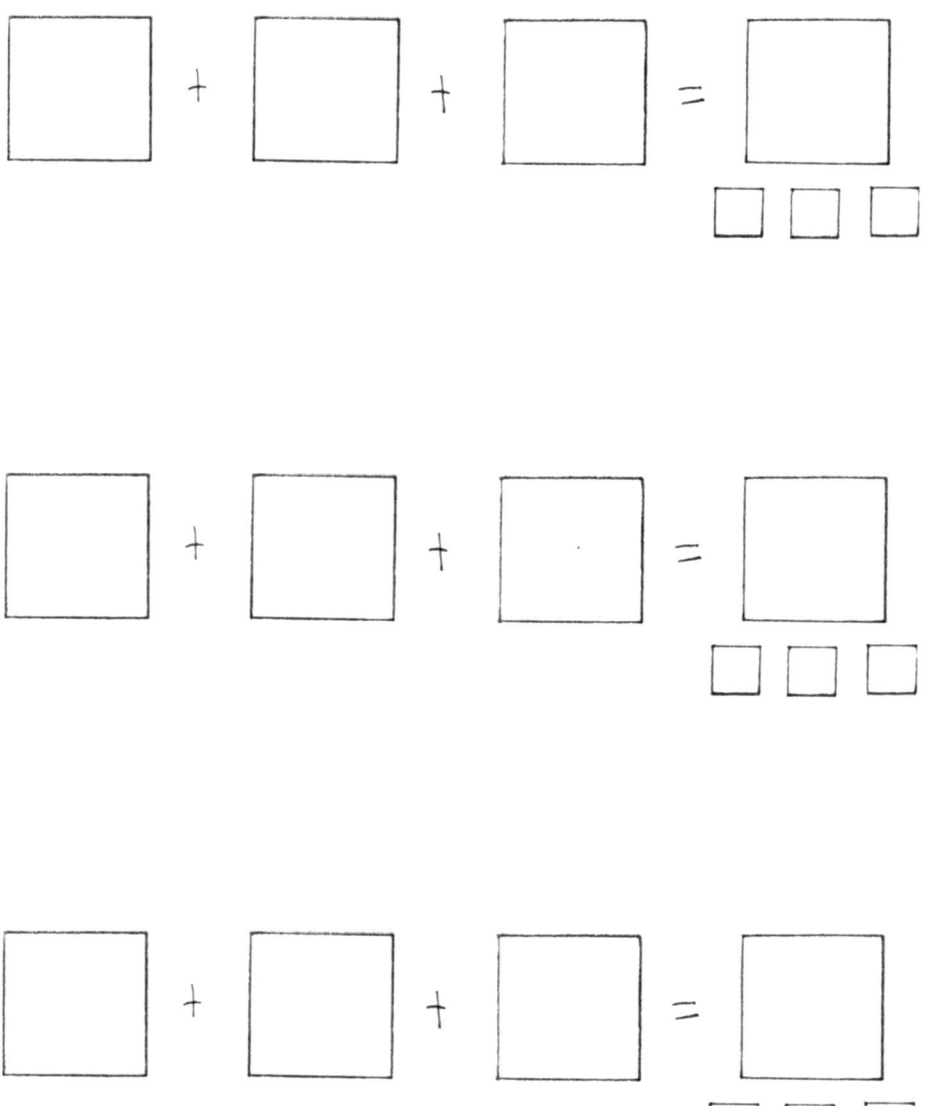

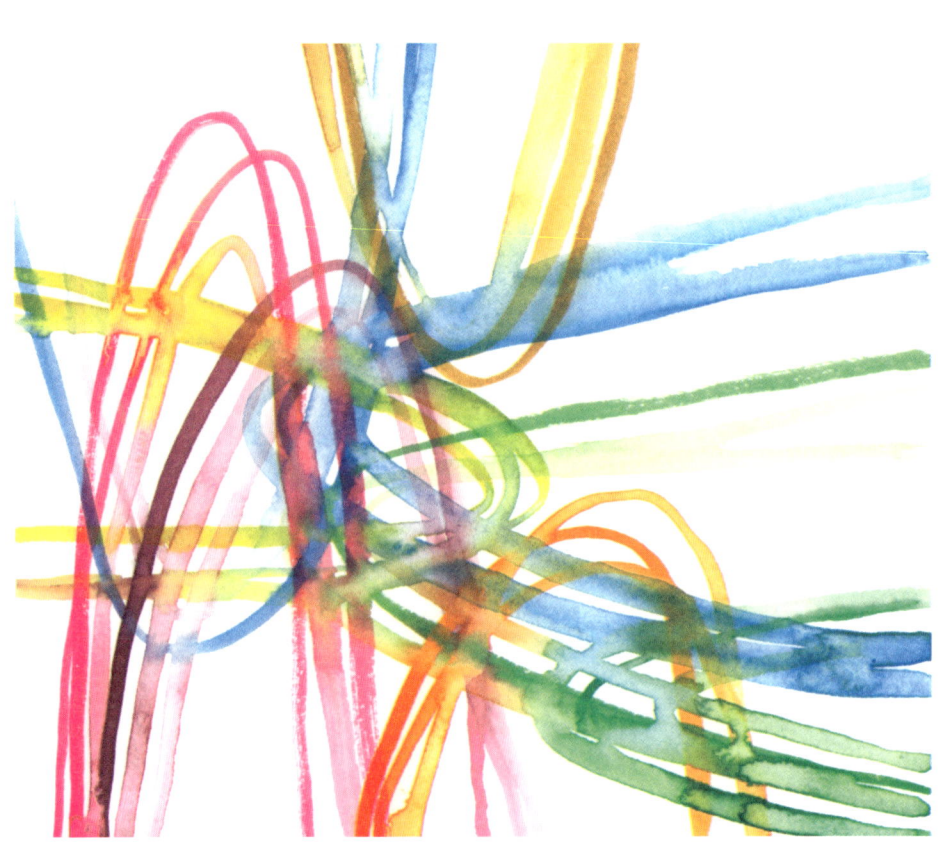

Color Meditation | **ARCHES**

I know you're probably thinking, isn't the arch a cousin of the rainbow? Or maybe even the direct brother or sister? You got me. But, to me, a rainbow has several stripes nestled up against one another and an arch is a singular mark. Semantics is a lovely thing, isn't it? I love making arches. The swoop your wrist and fingers have to make is so satisfying. See how it feels to make really big arches that fill the whole page versus really small arches. This effect is even cooler if you use a huge brush versus a tiny brush. Do them fast, do them slow, do them with your eyes closed.

▸ Paint some arches

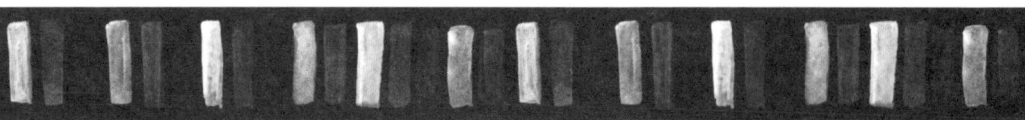

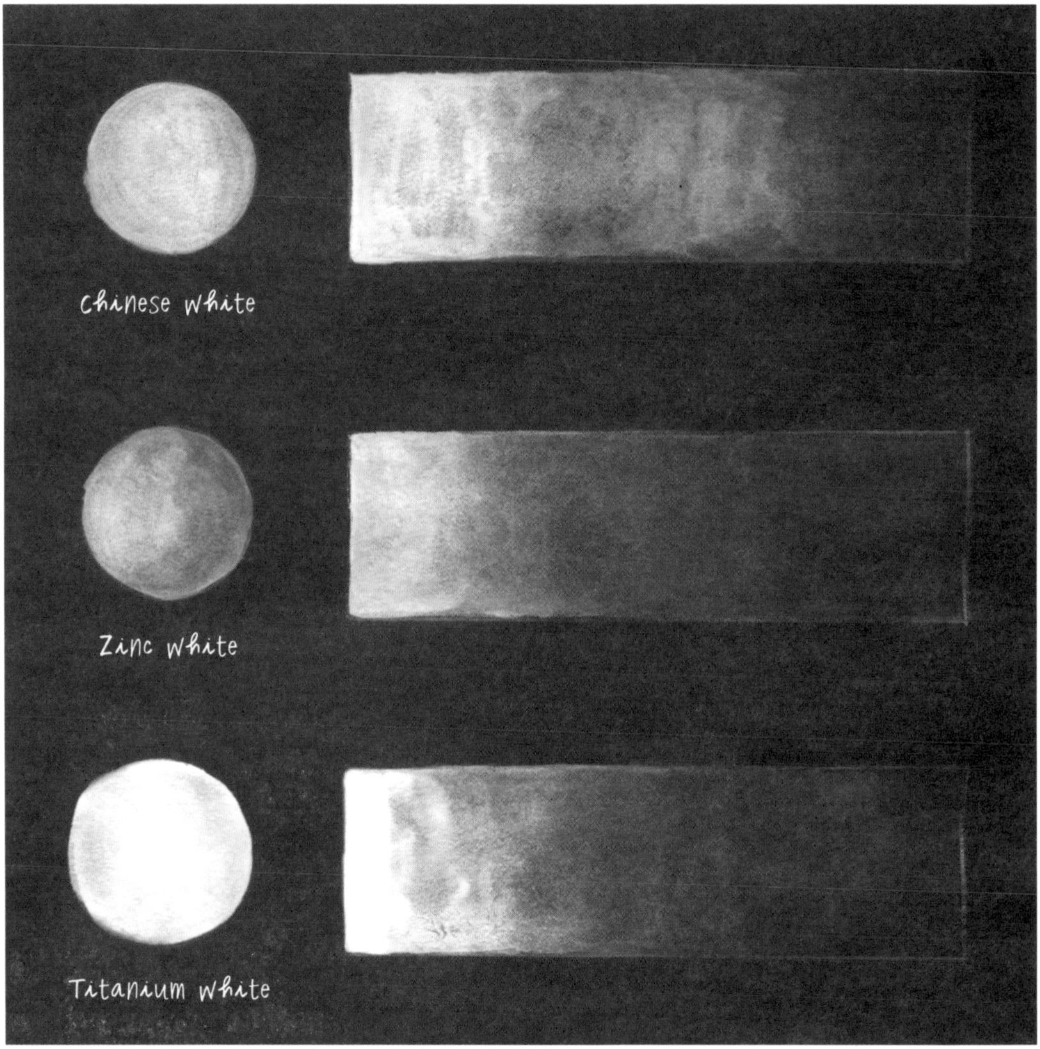

Chinese white

Zinc white

Titanium white

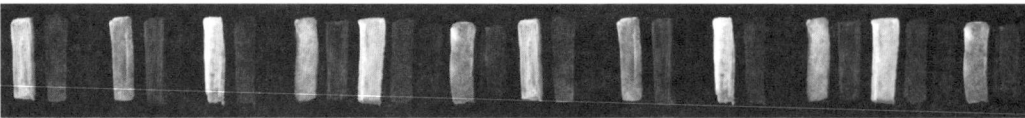

8.

WAIT, THERE'S MORE THAN ONE KIND OF WHITE TOO?

Yes, there's more than one kind of white! There are two main whites available in most paint brands, but there are a couple others I'll mention here for good measure too. Remember each company has slightly different formulas, but here are the general whites available.

TRANSPARENT MIXING WHITE / ZINC WHITE

- These two whites are usually pretty interchangeable. Also Chinese white in watercolor and gouache is more like these whites.

- They were developed to replace lead/flake white and have similar properties. (Purists might disagree with this; there are some people who want lead in their white, but I want fewer, not more toxins in my paint.)

- They're transparent in nature—meaning you can see through them—thus they're great for tinting. These whites allow the main hue to keep more of its vibrancy than other whites, which means they make less pastel-like colors.

TITANIUM WHITE

- This is the powerhouse of whites. It's *white, white, white*—if you want that bubblegum pink, you need this.

- It's very opaque (and thus good for covering).

- It's currently the most popular of whites.

- Note that it often comes in various formulas: bleached versus unbleached (which will be more yellow and creamy).

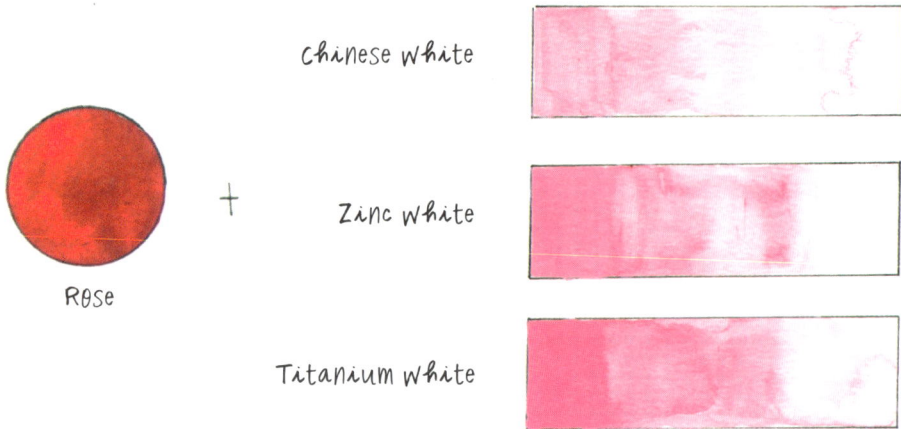

Chinese White

Zinc White

Titanium White

Rose

BLENDS

Some paint brands offer a blend of different kinds of white. Be sure to check swatches or color charts so you can see and understand their properties.

GOFUN SHIRAYUKI

This is an old Japanese white that is made from ground oyster shells. Some claim that this white is more luminous than others. If you've tilted an oyster shell in the light you can guess how this might work. Some painters really love it for its versatility because it's known to act both like a transparent and an opaque white. If you create your own paint (mixing straight pigment with a binder), which you generally have to do with Gofun as it isn't readily available in a commercial tube, you'll eventually end up with two layers of paint: a top, more transparent, layer and a bottom, more opaque, layer. You can mix these and/or use these together, or you can keep them separate for different types of white applications. The opaque will cover better and make more pastel colors; the transparent will shift a hue less and will layer on top of another color.

CREMNITZ WHITE

This is usually only found in oil paints, and people claim it's the true replacement for lead white (which they swear has a different consistency than other whites). Some claim that lead/cremnitz white is also the most stable, meaning it stays a whiter white over the years. Titanium white and zinc white have been known to shift toward yellow, or to flake a bit more, although these days paint formulation is pretty darn good and these issues are not as concerning.

> **PRO TIP:** When it comes to using white, do *not* add white to your hue. You'll end up using so much white, and it may never get as pastel or tinted as you want. *Always* add your hue little by little to a pool of white. You'll have much more control and you'll see how a little bit of a hue goes a long, long way.

Pick one hue and add it in percentages to your white of choice to see how it all works. (If you like, grab a black piece of paper on which to complete this exercise.)

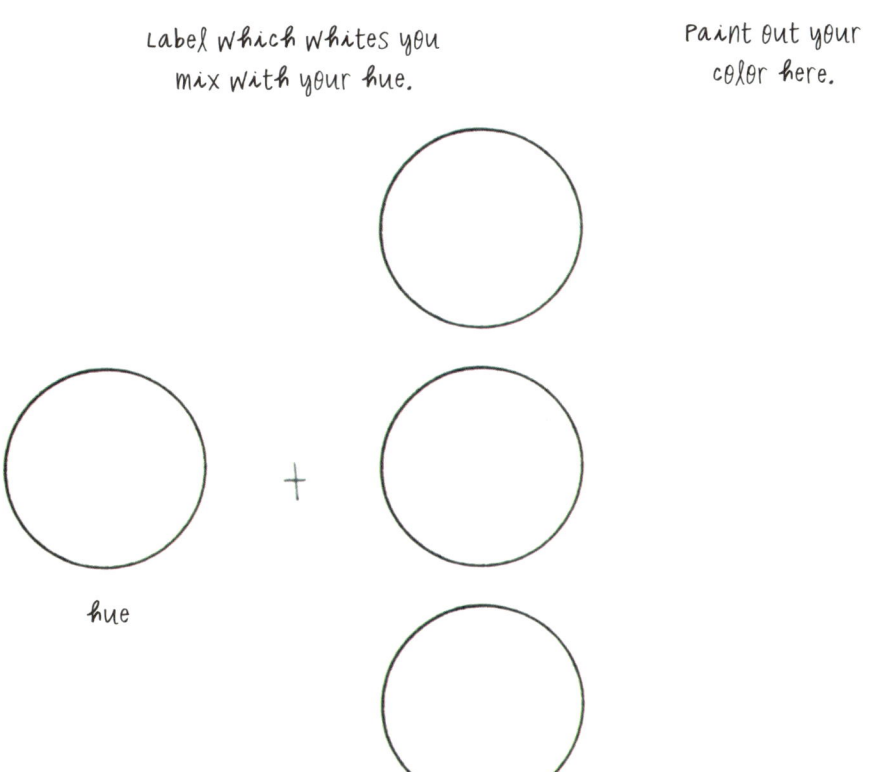

Label which whites you mix with your hue.

Paint out your color here.

hue

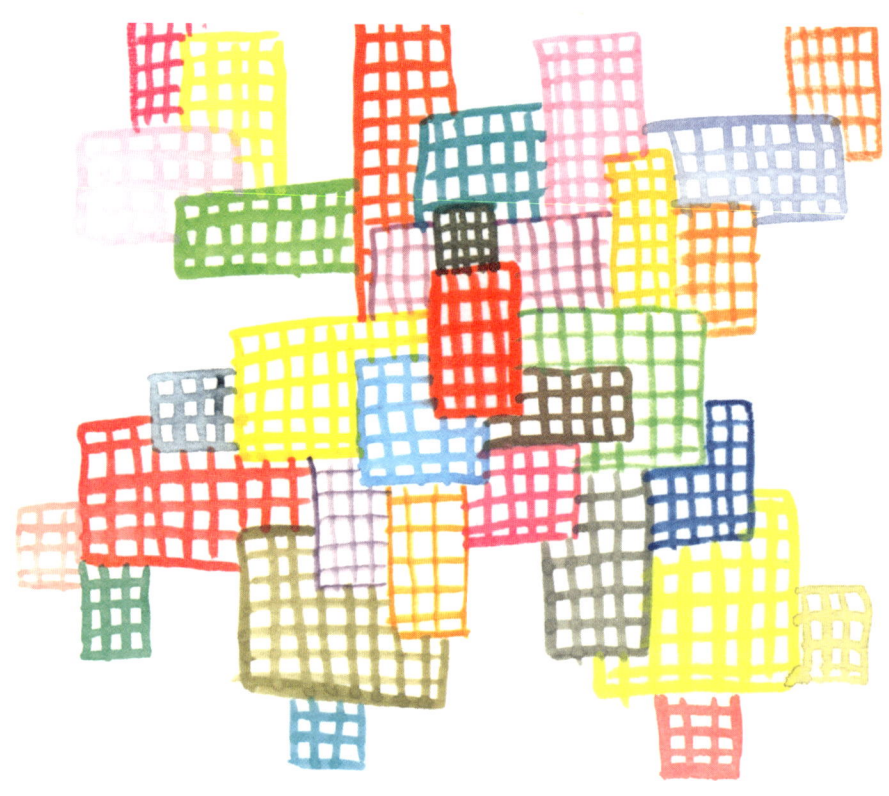

Color Meditation | **GINGHAM OR PLAID**

I love gingham. It's got a vintage vibe but always feels modern and fresh
to me. I also love plaid—the way interlocking colors work together. There's
usually a bright accent line in a plaid that kills me every time. (Oh hello,
unexpected yellow!) I've done color meditations loosely based on each of
these patterns. I was really thinking a lot about what happens when you use
one color and paint it on top of itself, because that's what happens in each
of these. Those darker spots in gingham are actually just two passes of the
same color. Think about stacking small areas of different colors of gingham
or make a plaid that goes across the whole page (and if you do, pick a good
accent color for me).

▶ Paint some gingham or plaid

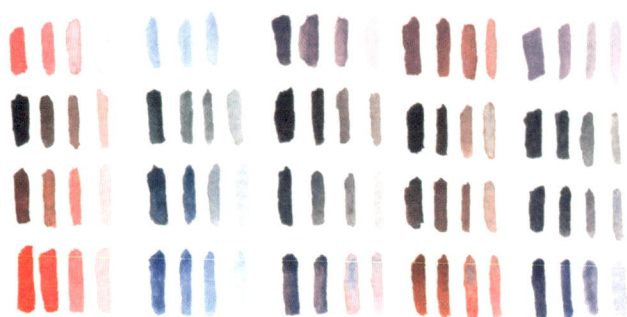

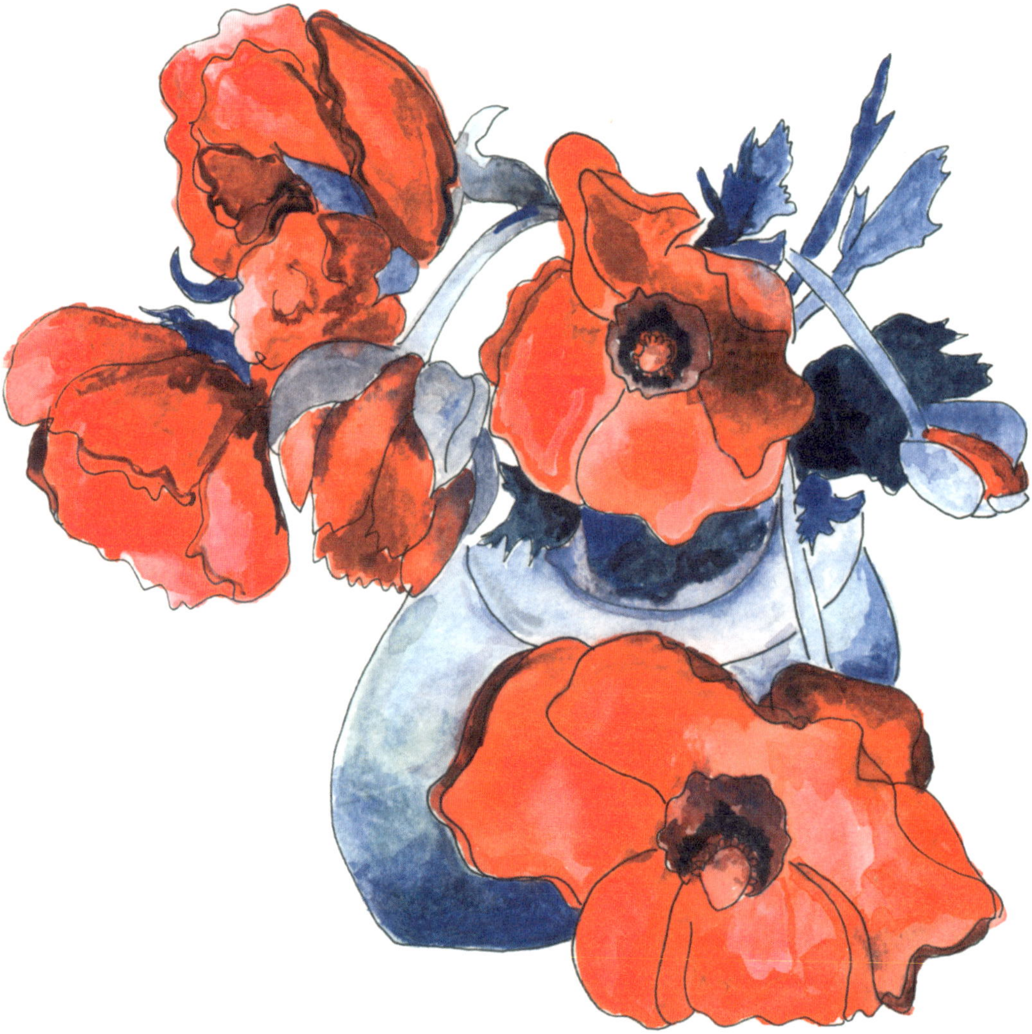

9. MIXING COMPLEMENTS

One of the biggest lessons you can learn in painting is the power of complements. As you made your shades for your color wheel I'm sure you noticed that adding black generates a very specific look. Often it seems rather unnatural. If you want to paint the shadows of a leaf or create a red that is just a tad darker but doesn't lean magenta, then you'll want to really understand how complements work.

You'll see I've taken the main complements purple/yellow, red/green, and two different versions of blue/orange and I've mixed them together. Technically, if you mix two complements in proportion you're going to get a mostly "neutral" color. This means it doesn't really lean warm or cool, and that it reads rather bland. You'll see that I've also painted the neutral out and then added it to the original hue to see how it affects it. It's pretty cool, isn't it? If you play more and more with complements, you'll be surprised by the diversity you can get. For example, purple/yellow in particular yields crazy greens and browns. If you add tints and shades, or even another hue, into the mix you can go on and on and on. In the span of a few minutes I was able to make thirty-three pretty distinct combinations.

In my beginning painting classes I often make students reproduce a painting that has a whole range of hues using four colors—a set of complements along with white and black. The students are always shocked at the range of colors they can get.

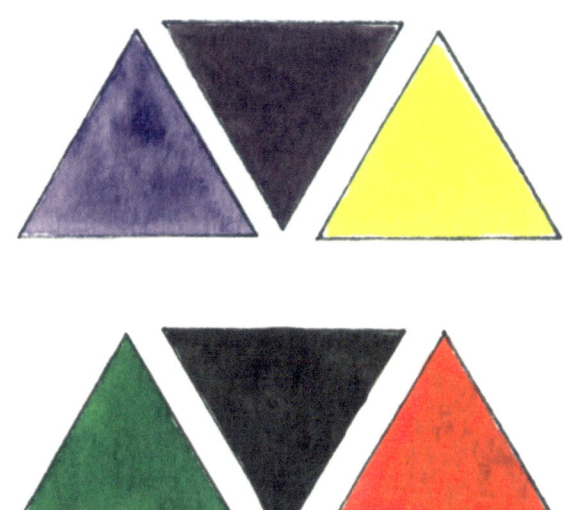

The center triangles in the above two sets have a 50/50 ratio of the two complementary colors.

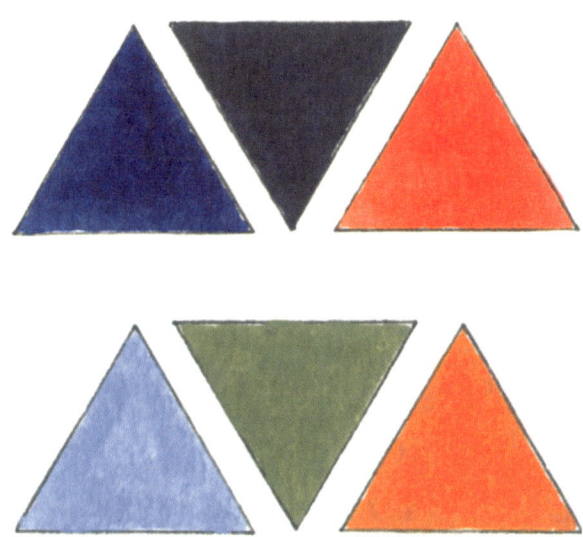

These combinations of complements are tints. Notice how their mixture in the center is also a tint and lighter than those above.

Use this space to try to make as many different hues, tints, and shades as you can using a set of complementary colors and black and white. Remember you can mix in any order: Add white to your yellow. Mix a yellow and black to make a weird green, and then add white or purple . . . GO CRAZY.

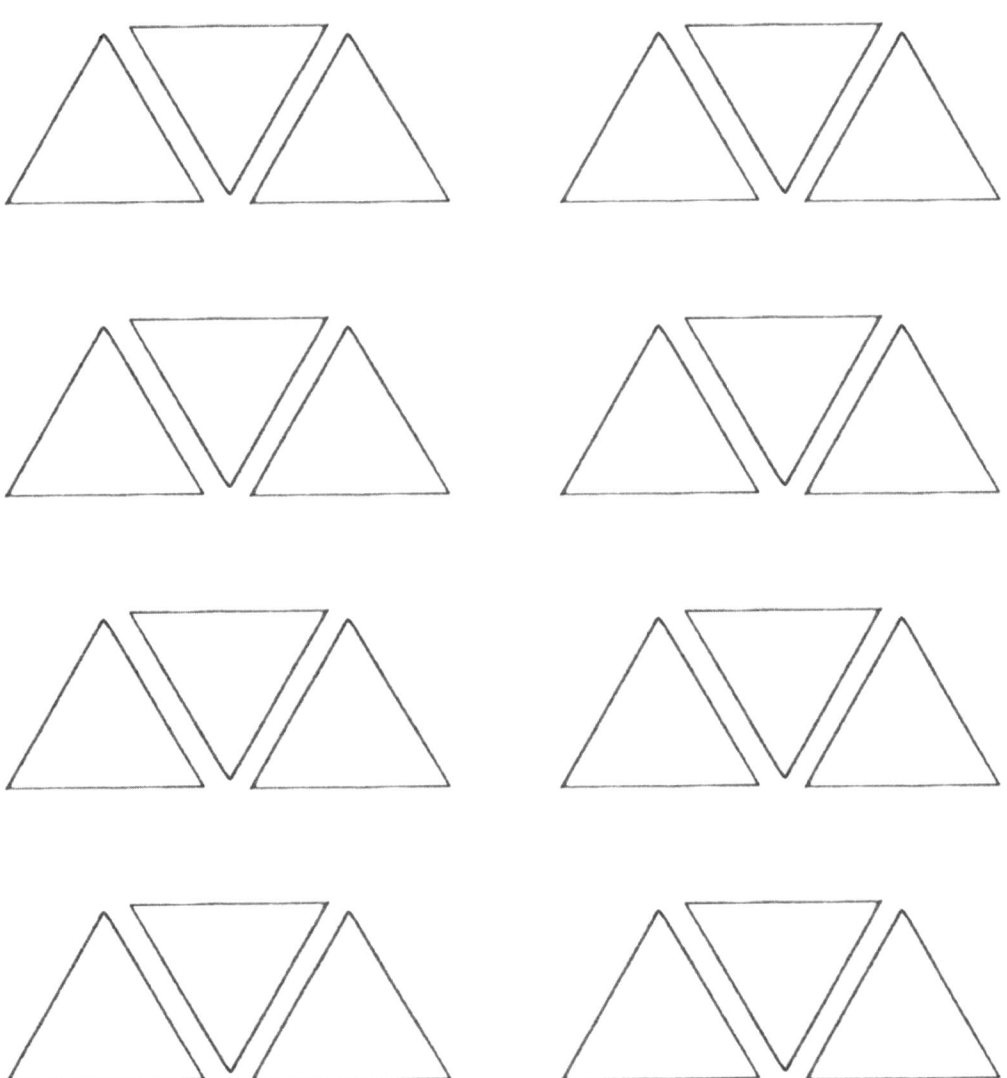

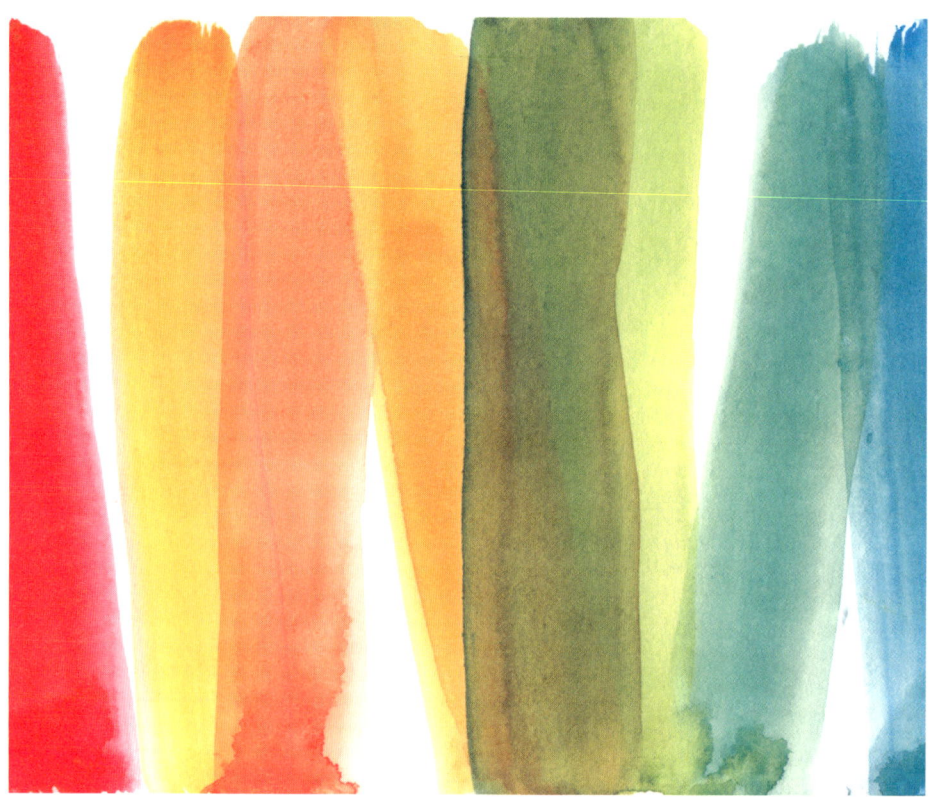

Color Meditation | **WASHES THAT OVERLAP**

Let's build on the overlapping color idea. One of the beautiful things about water-based paint is that it's easy to make washes—just add water. These washes are transparent and interact with each other to create new (and sometimes unexpected) colors. If you've never given yourself permission to just play with washes, now is your moment. Do it! If you don't want your colors to bleed make sure you let each wash dry before overlapping it. If just experimenting with overlapping washes isn't enough for you, use different brushes too, and learn what they can do. For my piece, I practiced with a big mop brush. Double whammy.

▸ Paint some washes that overlap

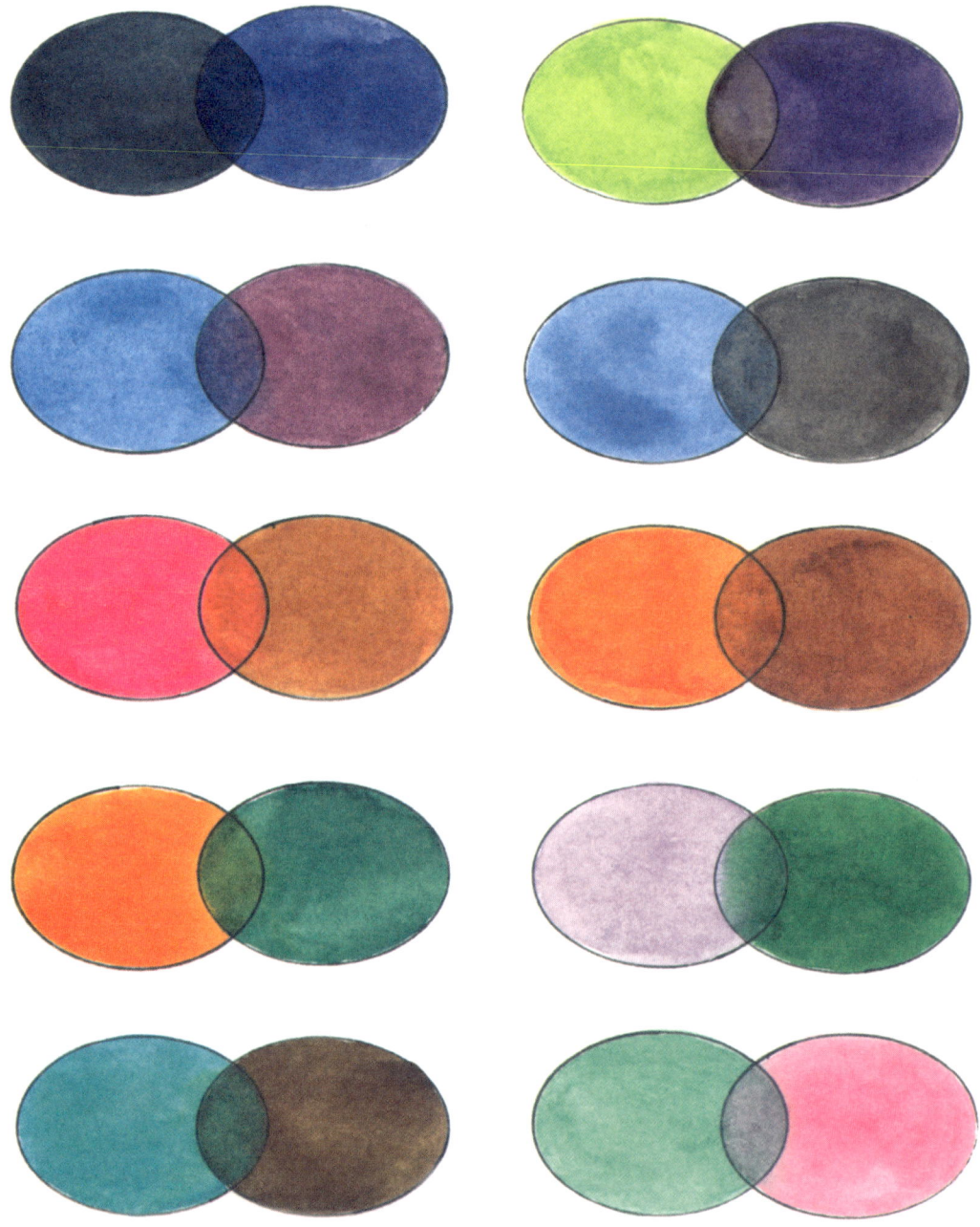

10. FAVORITE COLOR VERSUS LEAST FAVORITE COLOR

One thing that always changes for me is my favorite color, but I think I might have a favorite in each hue around the color wheel. While we're often aware of the colors we like, it's equally important to know what colors we do *not* like, and to not stay away from them just because we do. We shouldn't avoid a color just because we don't like it. Sometimes the colors we least like on initial sight can still be useful in color mixing, or our perception of the color can actually change when surrounding colors or light shift. This exercise is meant to push your ideas about favorite and least favorite colors and to see if maybe they can get along. They might not, and that's OK too.

I've painted several versions of favorite colors of mine—some are straight out of the tube, some are mixed. In some of these I've done my favorite and least favorite of the same hue—green, blue, purple. Where the ovals overlap I wanted to see what happened when the colors overlapped. (It's easier to make this work if the first color is dry before you go over it with the second color.)

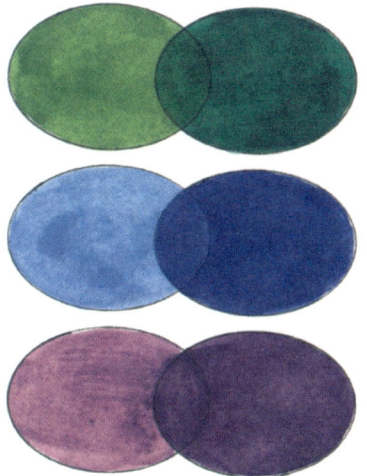

I also took a favorite and least favorite color and made a tint and shade to see if it changed how I felt. It definitely did about my least favorite muddy red-brown color—I like it much more both as a tint and a shade!

Favorite color with tint and shade

Least favorite color with tint and shade

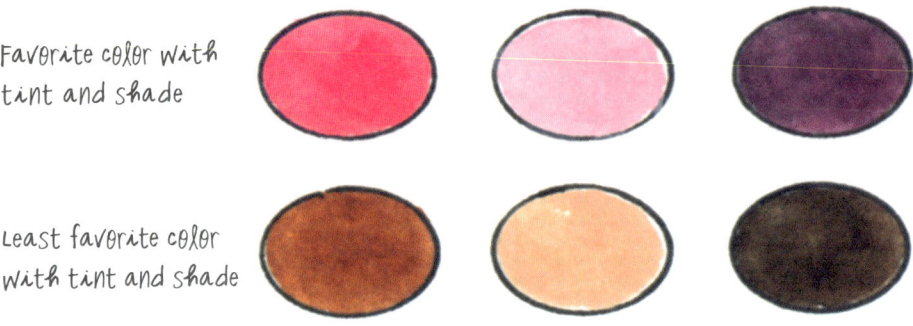

Your turn! Don't forget to mark which is your favorite and least favorite.

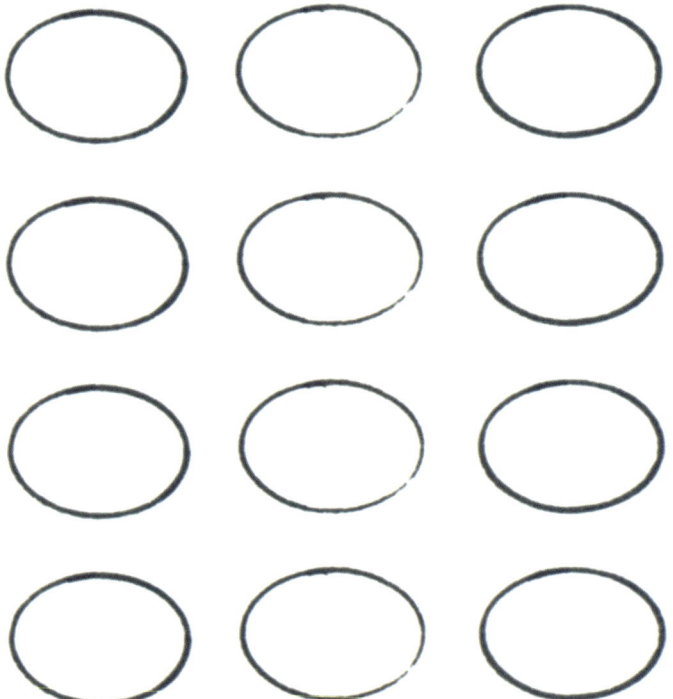

Mix your favorite and least favorite colors:

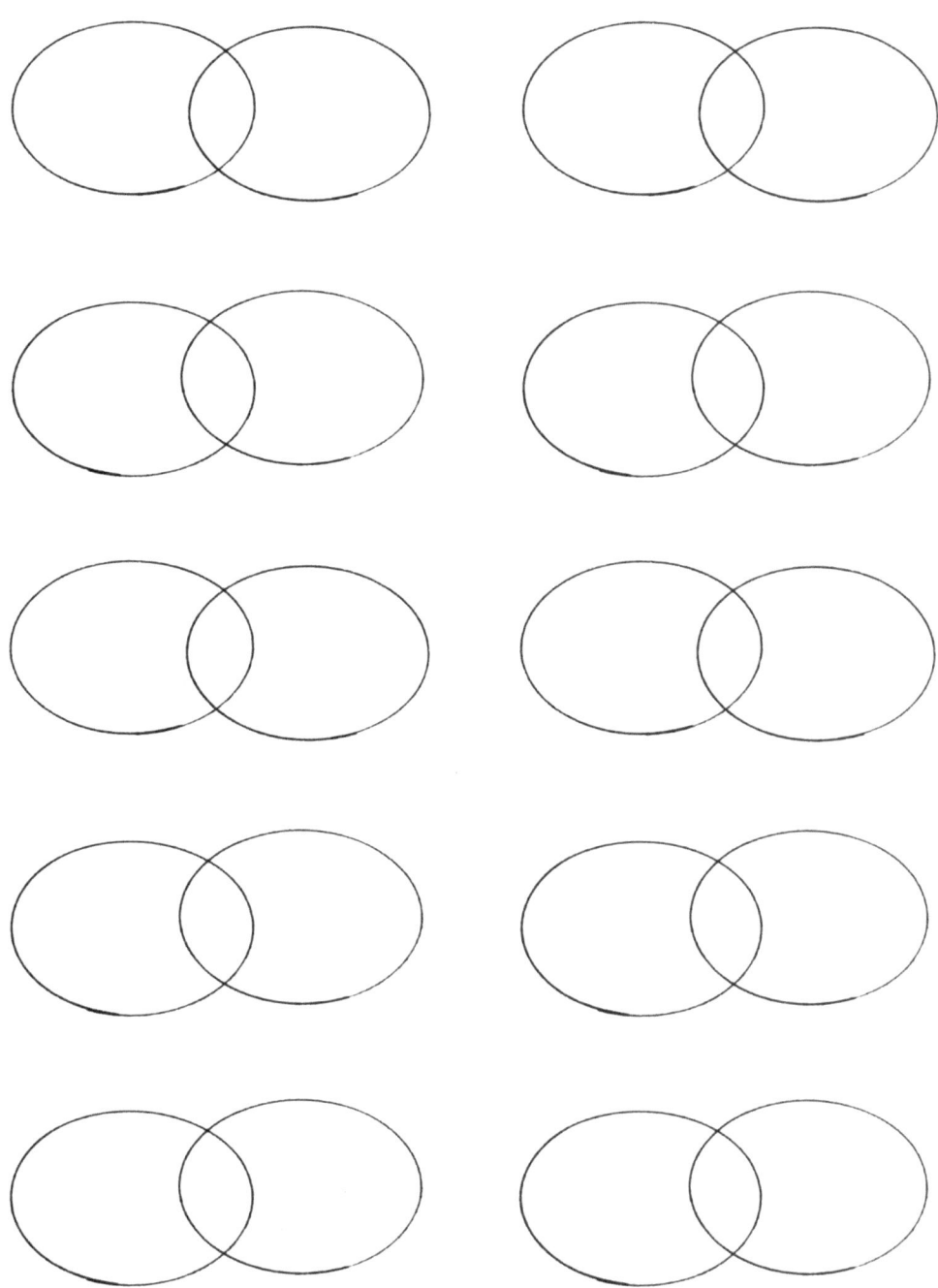

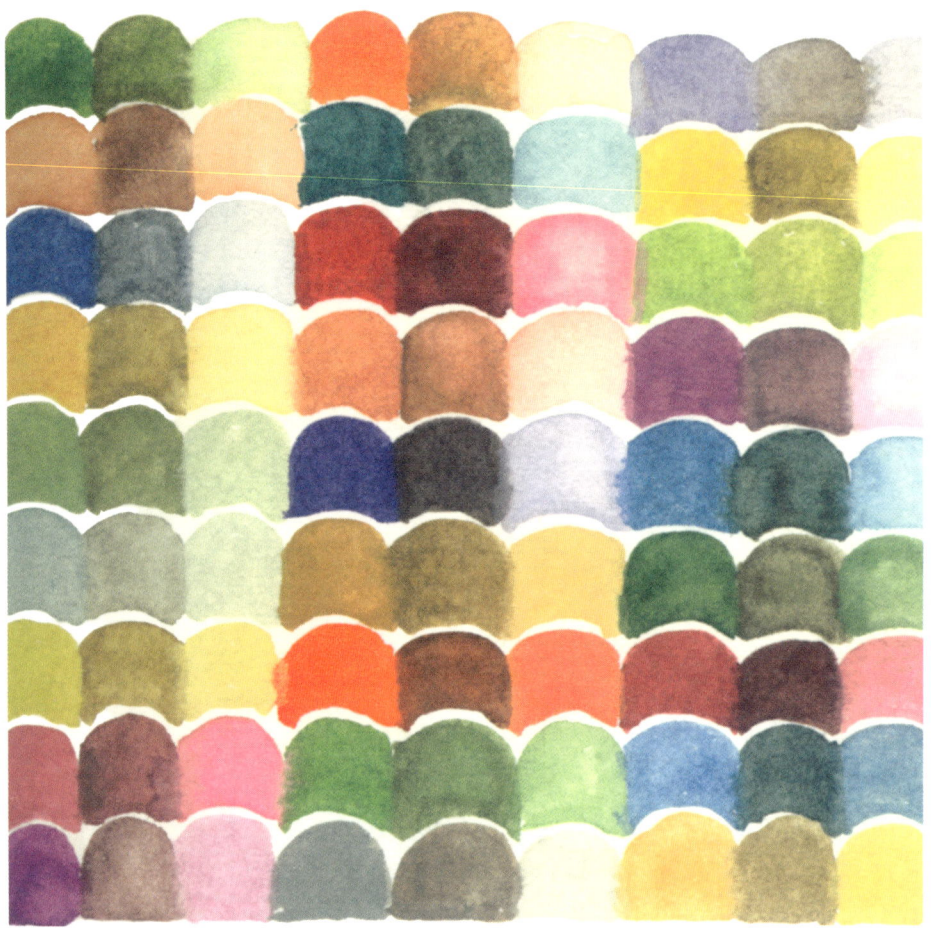

Color Meditation | **INSPIRED BY**

I don't know about you but I get inspired by the most random things that I look at throughout my day. Some seem more obvious than others—flowers, plates, the packaging of just about anything, LEGO bricks, EKG lines, someone's post about something somewhere... Take that visual inspiration and turn it into something you can repeat and do a color meditation. Mine is a rack of paint chips at the hardware store.

▸ Paint something you are inspired by

Cherry
kiwi chew   Orange   Lemon

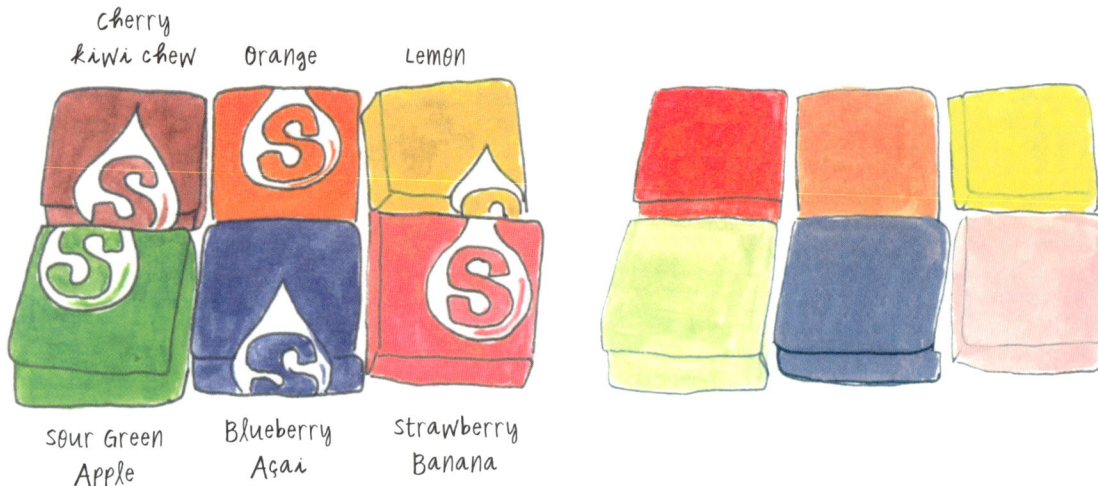

Sour Green   Blueberry   Strawberry
Apple   Açai   Banana

Sour   Piña   Mango
Cherry   Colada   Melon

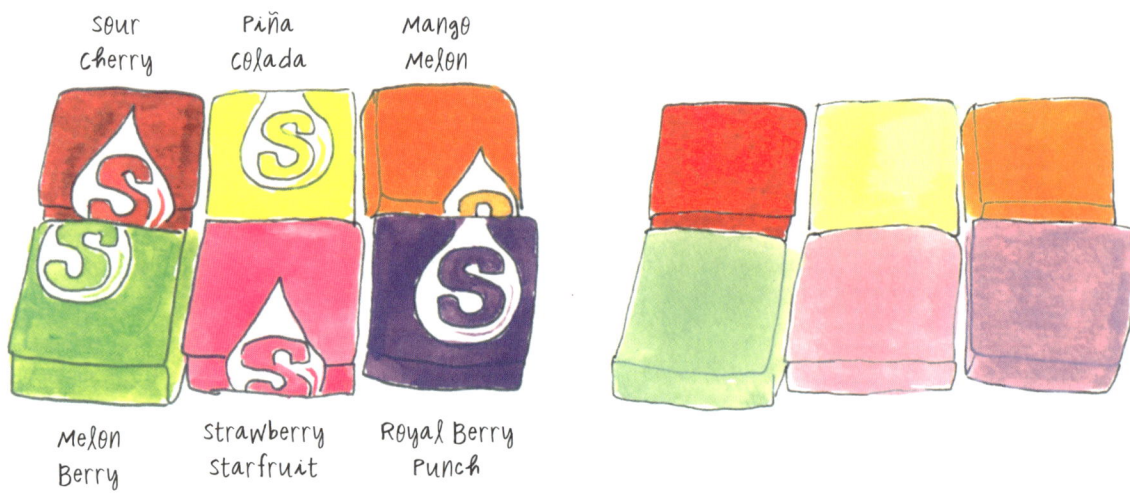

Melon   Strawberry   Royal Berry
Berry   Starfruit   Punch

11. STARBURST COLOR MATCHING

This is my all-time favorite student prompt (I mean, ever). Color matching is *hard.* In a room full of twenty students there's usually one student for whom this exercise takes thirty minutes to an hour; everyone else struggles for up to three hours to color match correctly. Here's the thing: It's an accomplishment to make a color you like. It's a greater accomplishment to be able to remake that color—again and again. *Exactly.* Take into consideration how things dry darker, how different papers and surfaces affect the paint, and how lighting changes—there are so many variables that might alter your color. Color matching is definitely a learnable skill, though. And one of the best ways to learn is to practice, practice, practice.

One of my favorite ways to practice is to match Starburst candies—the wrapper *and* the candy. Why? Because so many of them are off—your set of twelve basic paints will most likely not make the right match straight. You're going to have to add a tad of something. The candy itself looks like you just need to add white, but that rarely does the trick. It's an illusion. Plus, I always promise my students that if they match correctly they can eat the candy (although often they've painted on top of the candy and shouldn't eat it anymore, so I give them a clean one). Use that as a reward for yourself for matching my version of the Starburst candies, or go out and buy your own and match to your heart's content.

If you have Starburst candies on hand, match those (or if you want an excuse to go buy some . . .). You can also match to my samples, or to *other* candy you have around the house—I've tried jelly beans, Smarties, and Jolly Ranchers (but I'd avoid chocolate; it should be candy-colored candy for it to be useful color-theory-wise).

Passion
Fruit Punch

Citrus Slush

Sweet Blue
Raspberry

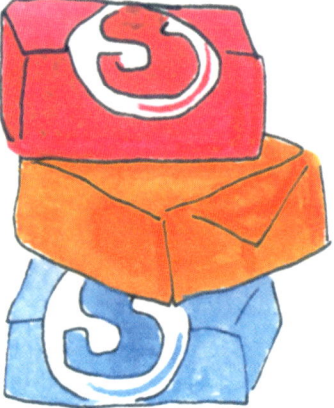
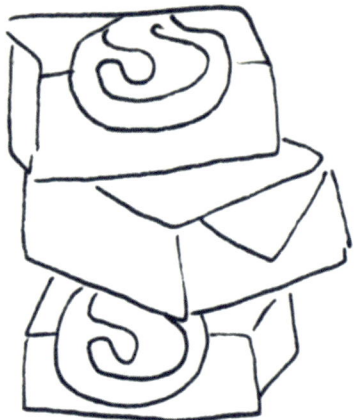

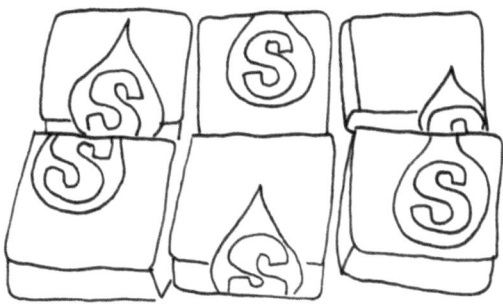 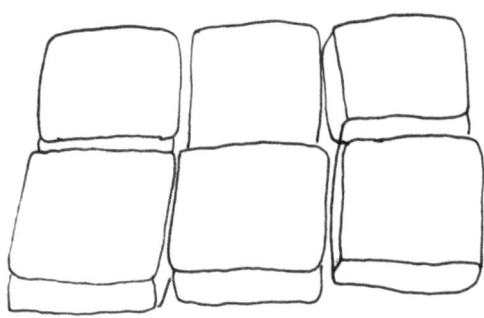

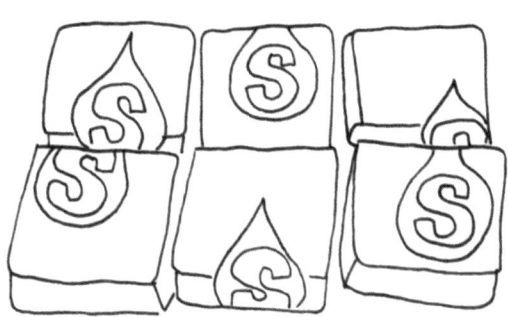 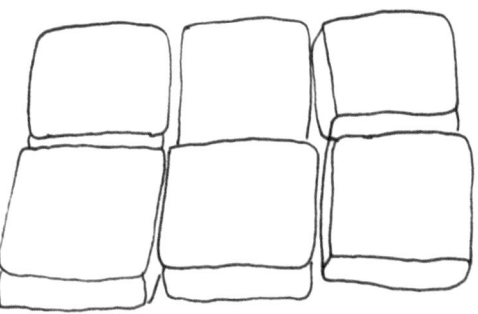

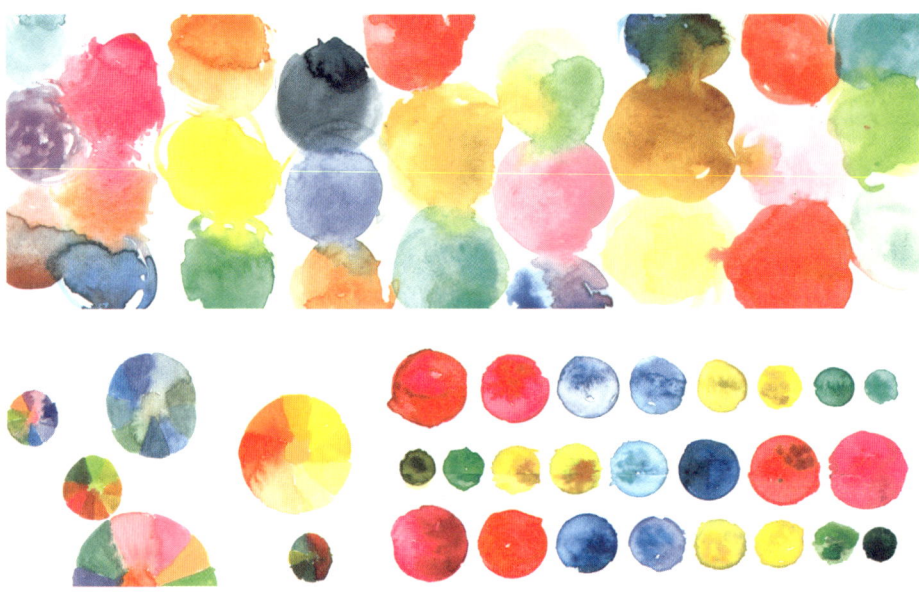

Color Meditation | **WET INTO WET**

What happens when you work wet-on-wet with wet media? Things you can't control. Things you don't expect. A weird mix of paint wonder. If you've done this before, then you know what I'm talking about. And if you have, then I suggest you push the limits of this technique. Can you re-create certain motifs or puddles of color? Is it even possible? Can you both allow the medium to do its thing while simultaneously exerting some control? If you haven't used this technique before, get ready. You can start with a dry sheet of paper or you can carefully place some water on your page. Watch what happens when you then add some color. Where does it move? It follows the water. What if there is more or less water? What if you blot? What if you get the whole page wet and work from there? (Be warned: this could be a mess, but we learn from our messes.) Try different degrees of wetness. What happens when you make a shape of one color and while it's still pooled and wet you add another color?

▸ Paint wet into wet

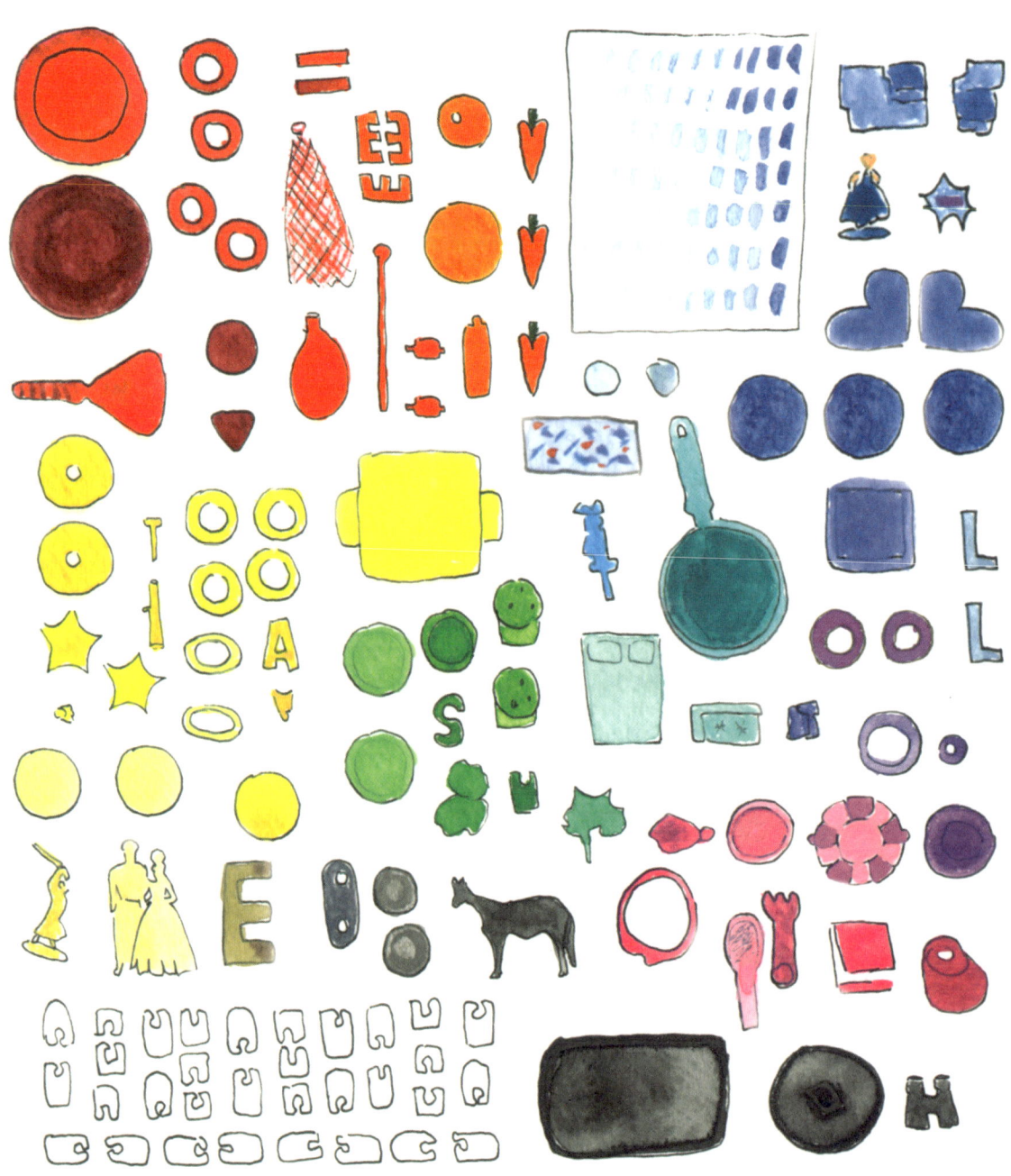

12.

ORGANIZE SOMETHING BY COLOR

Sometimes it's a good idea to step away from the paint and explore color inspiration elsewhere. There are things you can do in your daily life that will inform your painting practice. Do you like how things look when they're arranged by color? I do. And so does my color partner in crime, Christine Buckton Tillman. In fact, the two of us have spent hours upon hours arranging crowdsourced items from all over the world in a rainbow chromatic order. We called this installation *Chroma* and it filled a 12 x 26-foot space. Not only did we think about what constitutes a red but also how to transition smoothly from a bright, light red to a deep magenta to a brownish crimson. We asked people to send us piles of their mostly plastic junk. Each time we got a submission we arranged it in color order and documented it. This whole process actually taught me a lot about color. Sorting by color helps you notice when an aqua leans green or blue.

Look for something *you* can arrange at home. Books, your kid's toys, colored pencils, markers, crayons (dump them out of the box so they're a mess and rearrange them), hair accessories, jewelry, beads—you get the picture. Arrange the items of your choice by color. When I'm arranging items, I start by putting like colors together. So all the *reds* and all the *greens*. Within those subcategories I look to place things from light to dark or vice versa. I tend to like things in rainbow order, so I start with red on one side and move my way through orange, yellow, green, blue, and purple, and then add neutrals— whites, blacks, browns, grays. If a color is missing, don't worry, just skip it. If you like, paint your composition on the next pages or document it with a photo—print it out and tape it in!

▸ Paint your Organize by color composition here

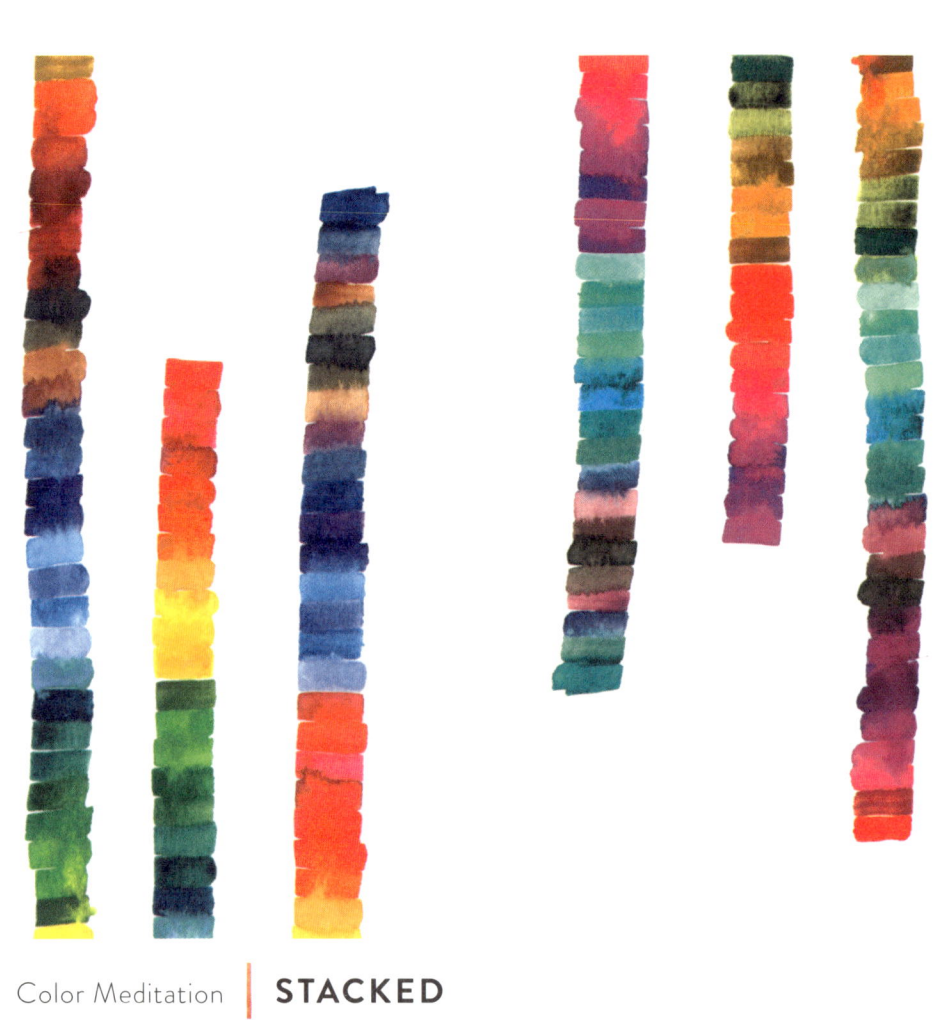

Color Meditation | **STACKED**

Things that are stacked are pleasing, aren't they? We're surrounded by stacks—products in grocery stores, books, towels on shelves. If you want to be overwhelmed by stacks, enter a big-box store or warehouse and look up. Take your favorite shape or mark that you've made thus far in a color meditation and stack it. Each stack can explore one color. The stacks can be the same size, they can be different, they can shift in saturation. By now you know the drill.

▸ Paint some stacks

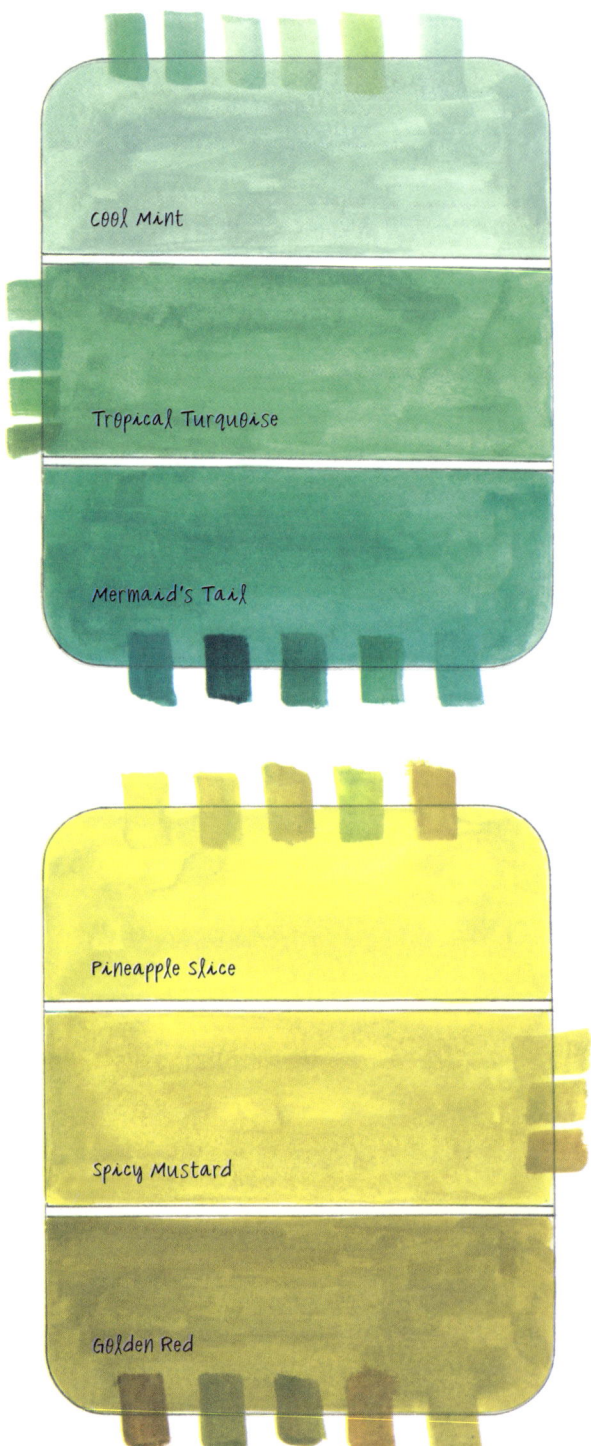

Cool Mint

Tropical Turquoise

Mermaid's Tail

Pineapple Slice

Spicy Mustard

Golden Red

13. PAINT CHIP MATCHING EXERCISE

I hope you liked the Starburst-matching exercise. You didn't have to pull out too much hair, did you? Let's try it again, but this time with paint chips, because, my goodness, if you have a color fascination you've probably stood in front of a paint chip display at a hardware store wide-eyed. I'll admit that I've been known to drool over them. And if I'm at a hardware store, a few always manage to make it into my pockets. Not only are they free but they're also really useful as color viewfinders. If you cut a square into them you can lay them over other colors to see if you like the combination!

Matching paint chips is also a really good way to learn about color—especially because most of them tend to offer three to four colors in a similar colorway per card. It's really easy to lay your paint chip down on a piece of paper and paint stripes onto it until you find your match! Below and on the next pages you'll see my versions of paint chips, each with a little oval for you to fill in. Feel free to paint swatches all around until you get the color right—then fill in that oval!

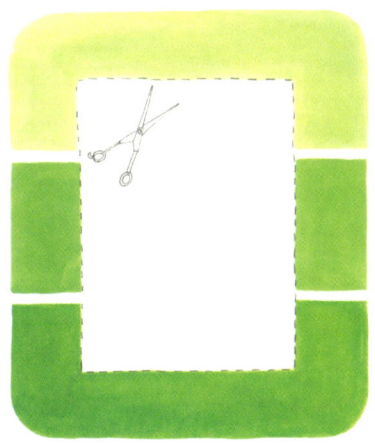

I love taking small paint chips & cutting squares out—they become viewfinders and you can use them for color tests.

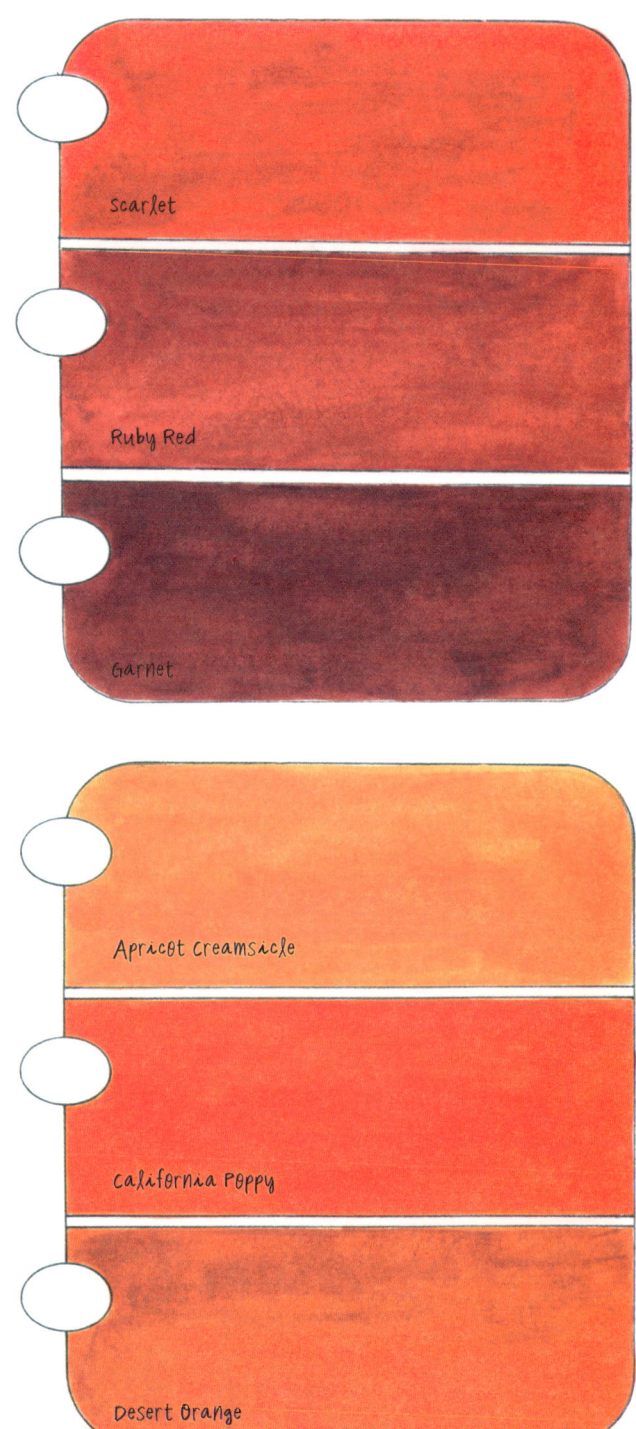

Scarlet

Ruby Red

Garnet

Apricot Creamsicle

California Poppy

Desert Orange

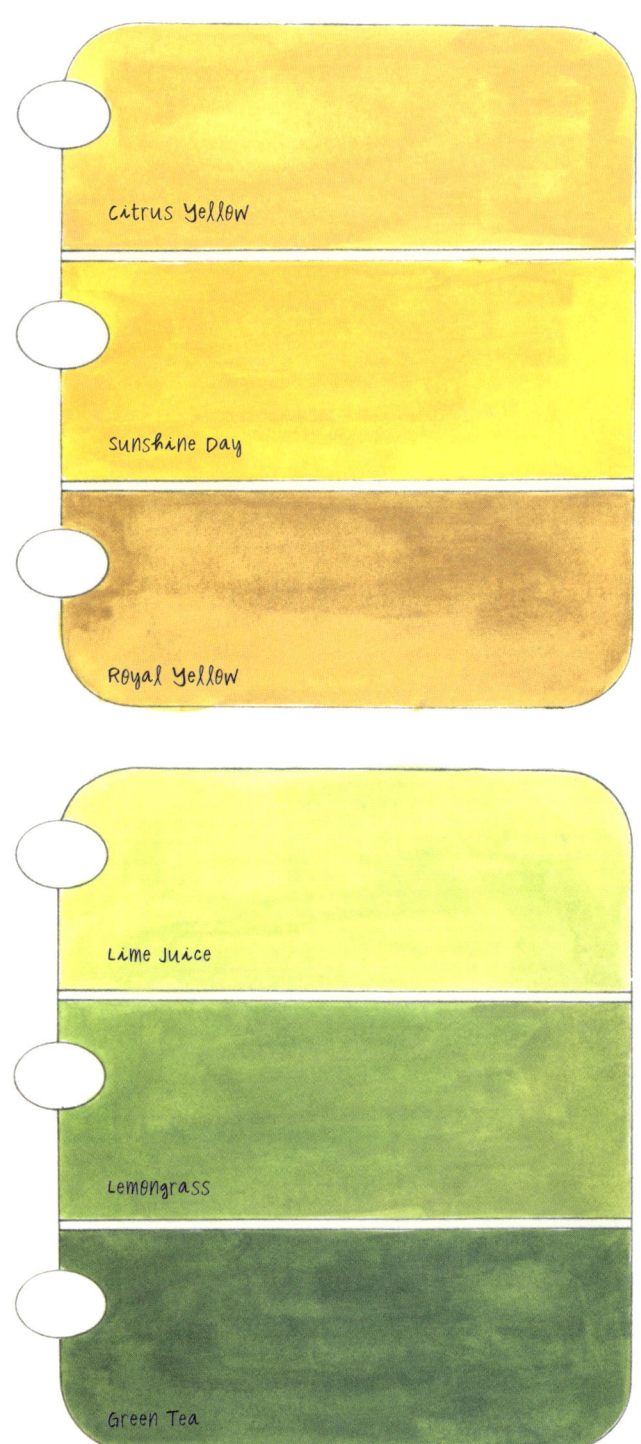

Citrus Yellow

Sunshine Day

Royal Yellow

Lime Juice

Lemongrass

Green Tea

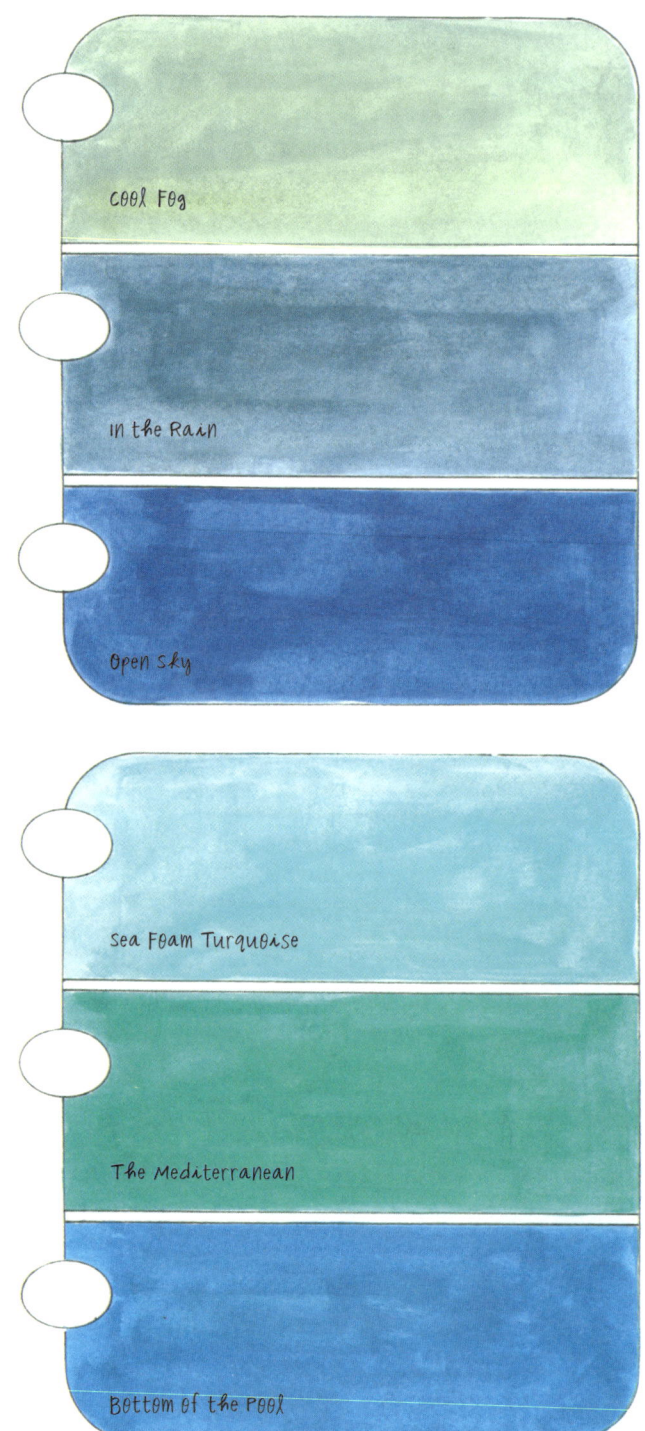

Cool Fog

In the Rain

Open Sky

Sea Foam Turquoise

The Mediterranean

Bottom of the Pool

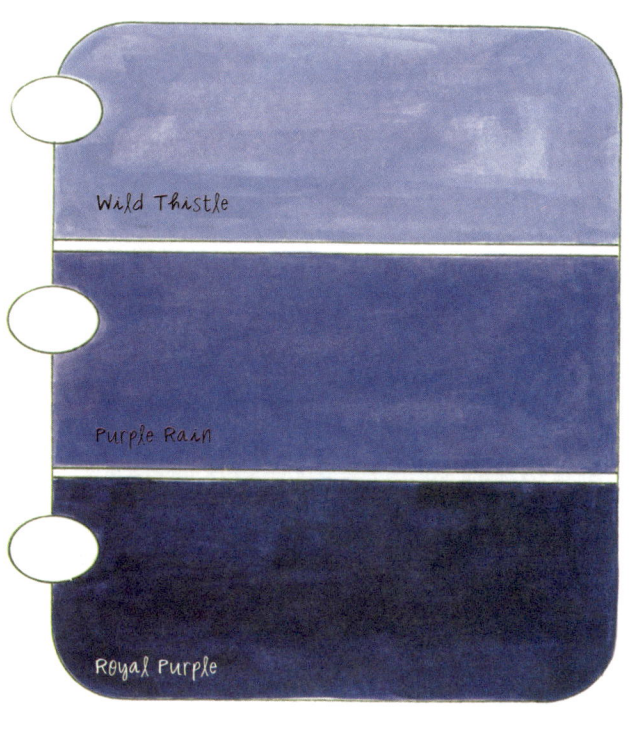

Wild Thistle

Purple Rain

Royal Purple

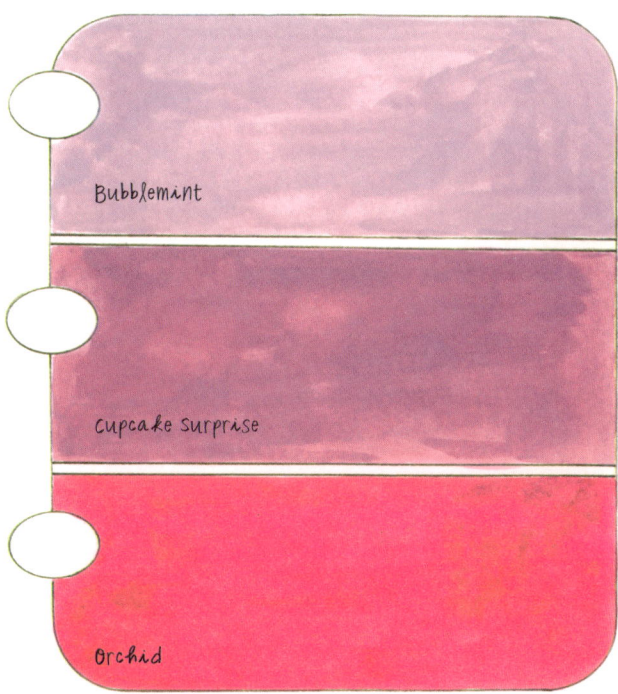

Bubblemint

Cupcake Surprise

Orchid

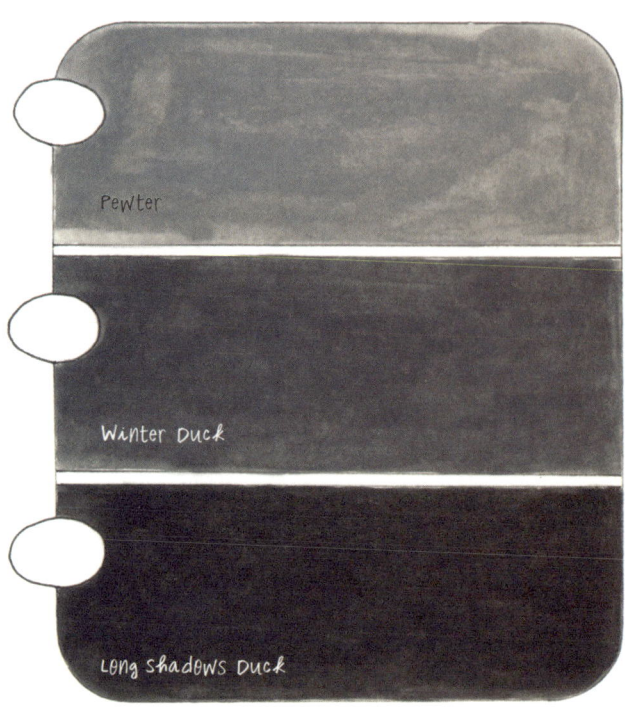

Pewter

Winter Duck

Long Shadows Duck

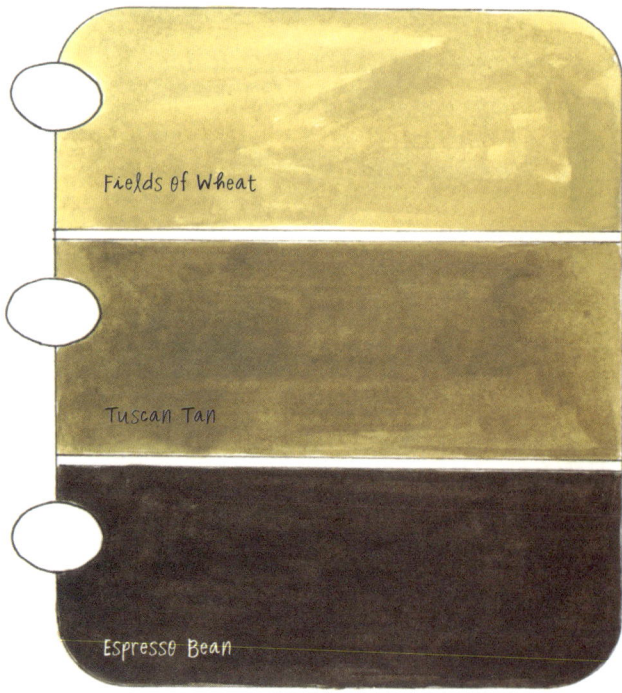

Fields of Wheat

Tuscan Tan

Espresso Bean

Go find a paint chip you like, tape it here, and match it!

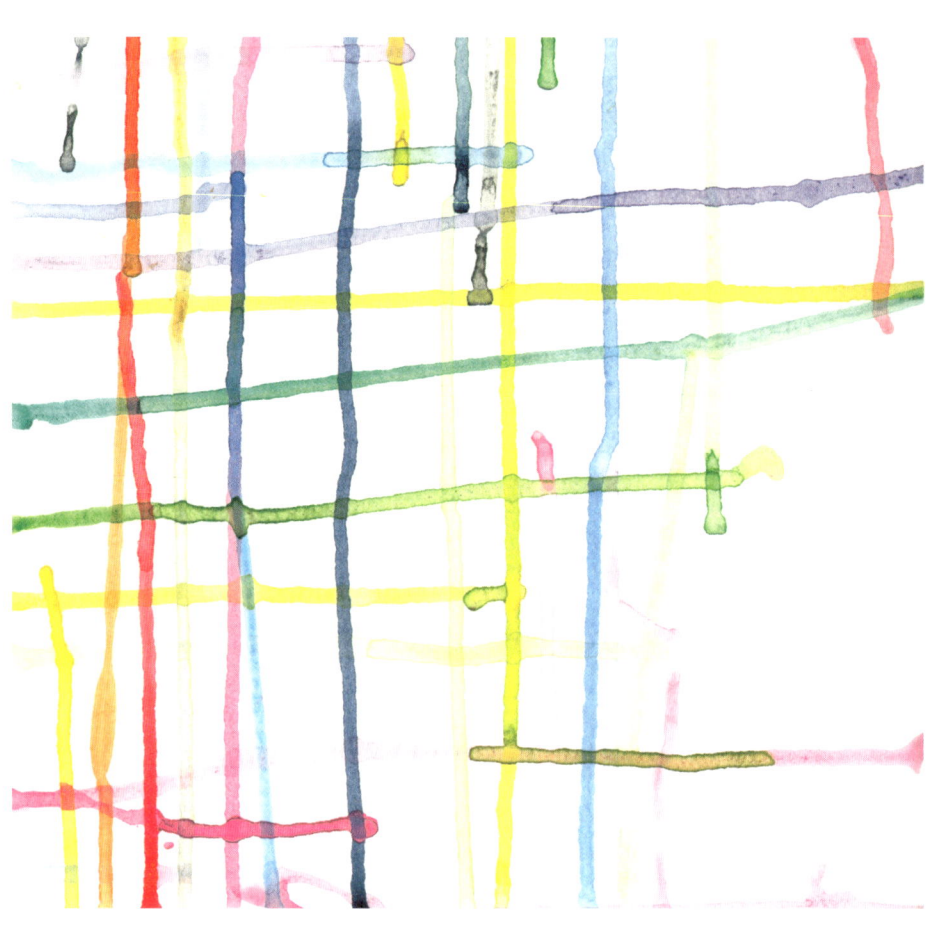

Color Meditation | **DRIPS**

Drips in wet media are fascinating—at least to me. They highlight that we're using water, and that we can both control and *not* control the way paint moves. The bigger the drop, the longer the drip—is that true? Do some colors drip better than others? Explore saturated drips versus desaturated drips, brush-driven drips versus dropper-driven drips. Move the book around while you drip; make them twist and turn. Alternatively, you can blow on a pool of paint and see if you can make it move like a drip.

▸ Paint some drips

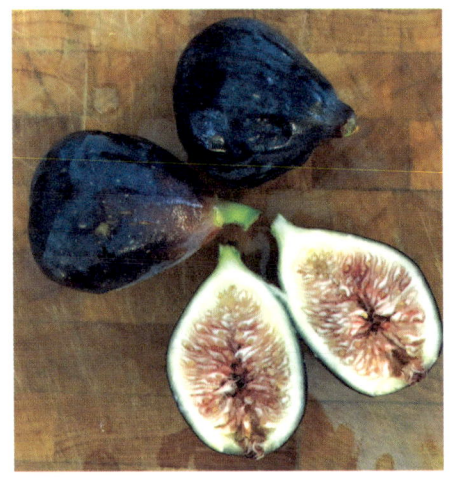

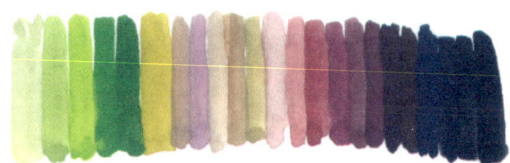

The colors of Figs

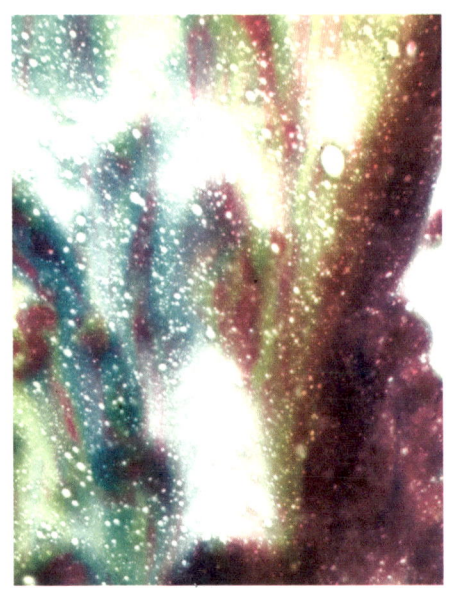

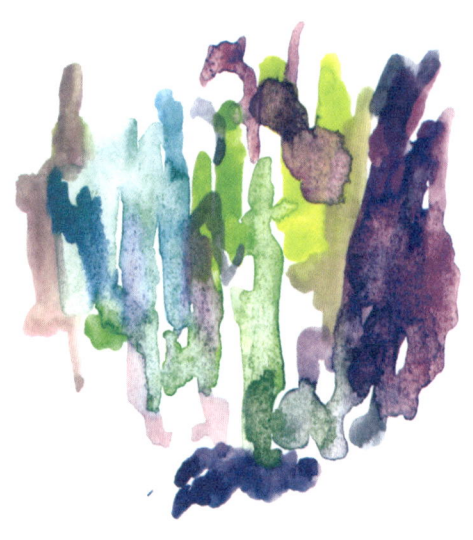

The colors of car-wash soap

14. OBSERVE AND DOCUMENT COLORS IN YOUR WORLD

I spent a year documenting the colors that surrounded me—I took a photo of something (anything) each day and then dissected the color from it in a quick study. It's a fun and simple way to learn about color harmony and color combinations. If you feel like you're stuck in a rut using the same colors for the same things all the time, then this exercise will not only help you be more observant but also hopefully force you to use and see colors you don't normally notice and/or think to use. Follow the prompts to find the colors in your world. There's no need to do elaborate sketches or be concerned with accuracy of shape. Simply create swatches based on what you see.

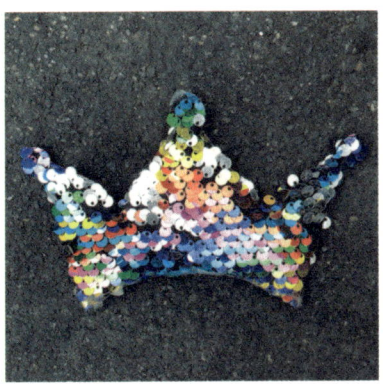

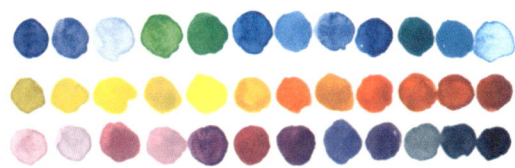

The colors of a sequin crown lost in a parking lot

The color of the sky for seven Days

The colors of a Flower or Bouquet of Flowers

The colors of something on your Desk

The colors of something from a Gumball Machine or a Toy

The colors of something you found

The colors of your Favorite Outfit

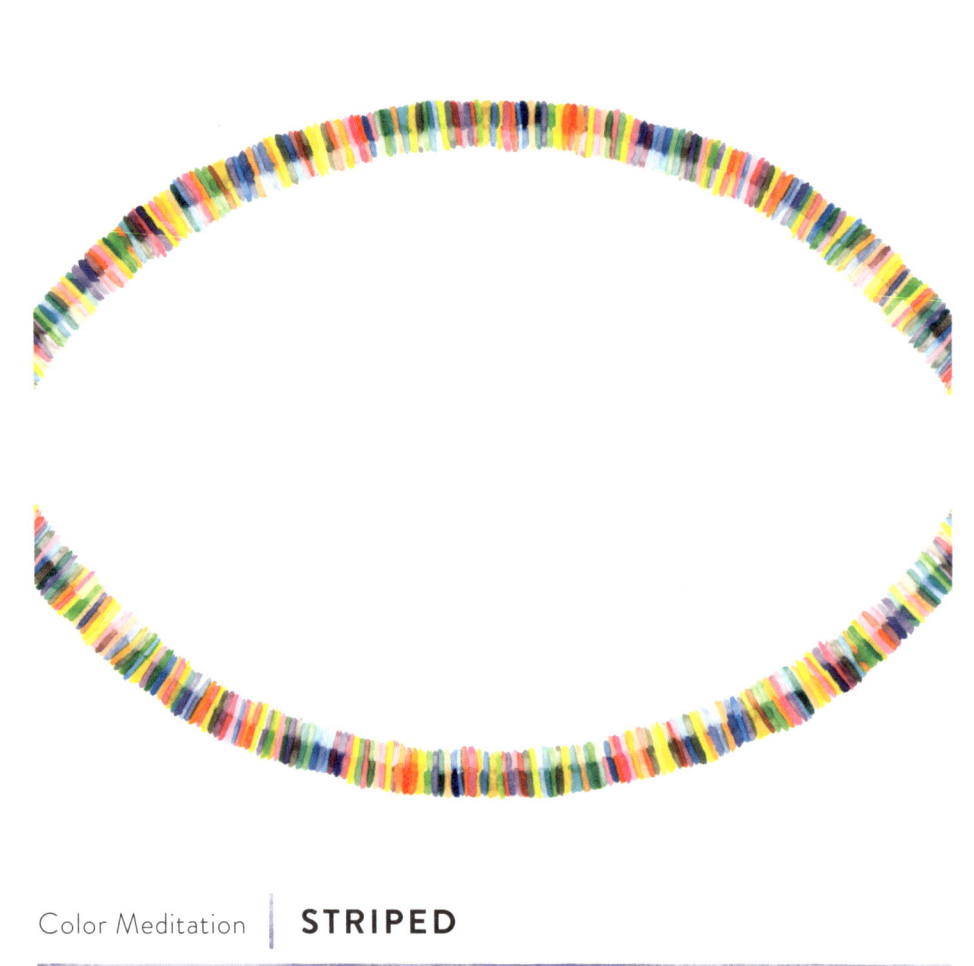

Color Meditation | **STRIPED**

I admit it: I love lines. So I had to come up with a way to use them again in a color meditation but not call them lines. So I'm calling them stripes. Make some stripes. Across the whole page. Inside a shape. All one color. In one million colors. Stripe to your heart's content.

▸ Paint some stripes

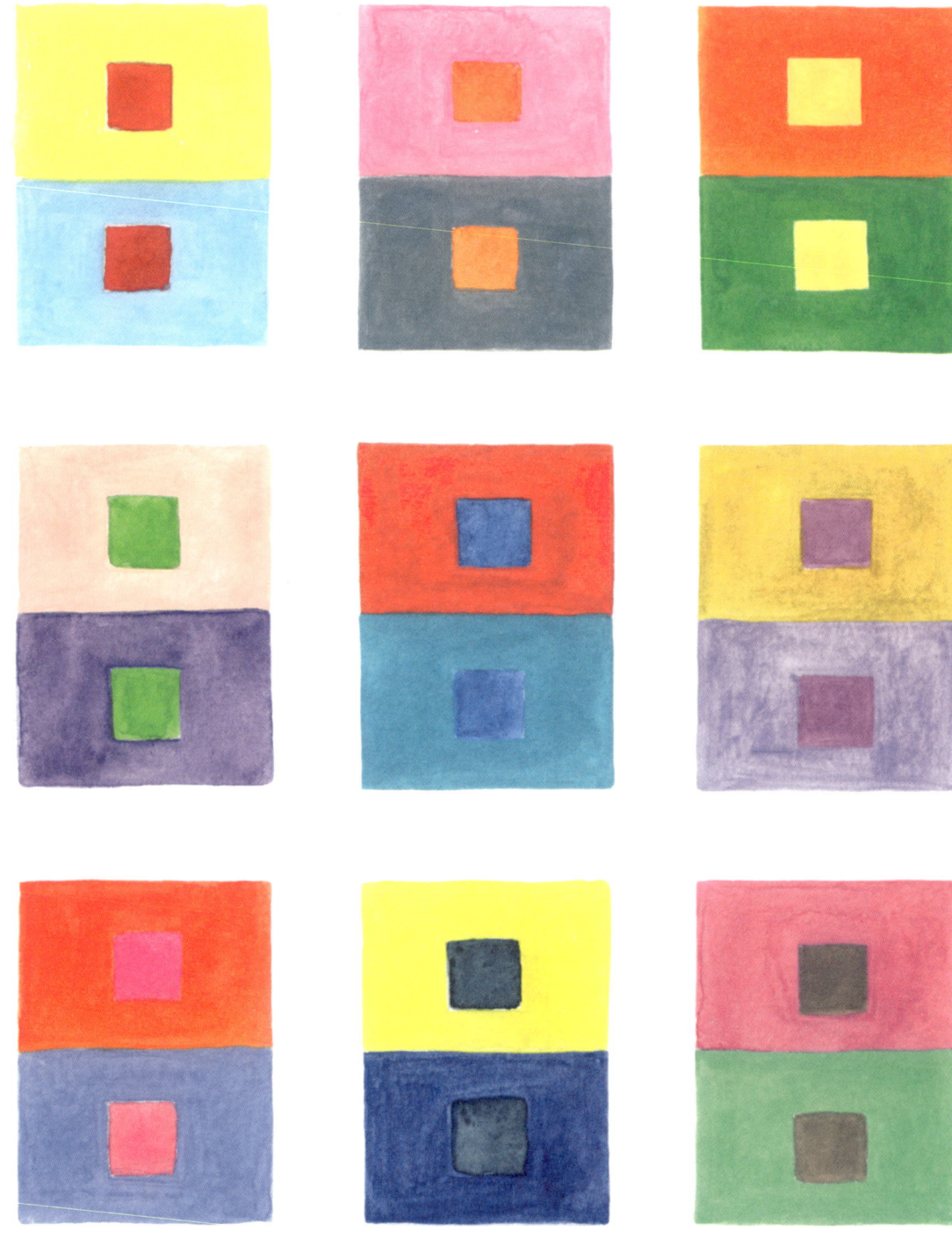

15.

LEVEL UP—INSPIRED BY JOSEF ALBERS

Josef Albers was an abstract painter, educator, designer, photographer, typographer, printmaker, and poet. If you want to take your color theory knowledge to the next level, make Albers's seminal book *Interaction of Color* your new best friend. I can't recommend it enough.

If I was going to distill one small nugget of information from Albers, it's that colors and how we view them are relational—that is, the same color will look incredibly different depending on the color that surrounds it. A lot of times students will ask me, "What color should I make this person's shirt?" I often counter, "You should figure out what color their pants and the background are going to be because color doesn't operate in a vacuum."

Hopefully this exercise will prove that, and then you'll get to have some fun impersonating Albers's square-within-a-square painting method too. In the small squares you'll place a color. Make sure it's the same color. Then pick two different colors to surround them. They can be complementary or any old color you wish. Watch how that surrounding color changes your reaction to the color in the small square.

For the square-within-a-square exercise, I suggest an exploration of one color from light to dark, or warm to cool, or paint the outside square one color and the inside square another and the middle square a fifty-fifty mix of the two.

Josef Albers

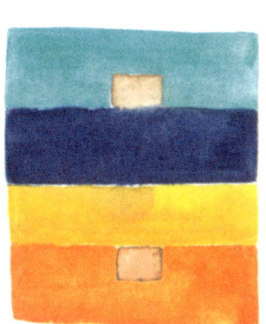

Interaction of Color
Unabridged Text and Selected
Plates Revised Edition

125

For the square-within-a-square exercise, I suggest an exploration of one color from light to dark, or warm to cool, or paint the outside square one color and the inside square another and the middle square a fifty-fifty mix of the two.

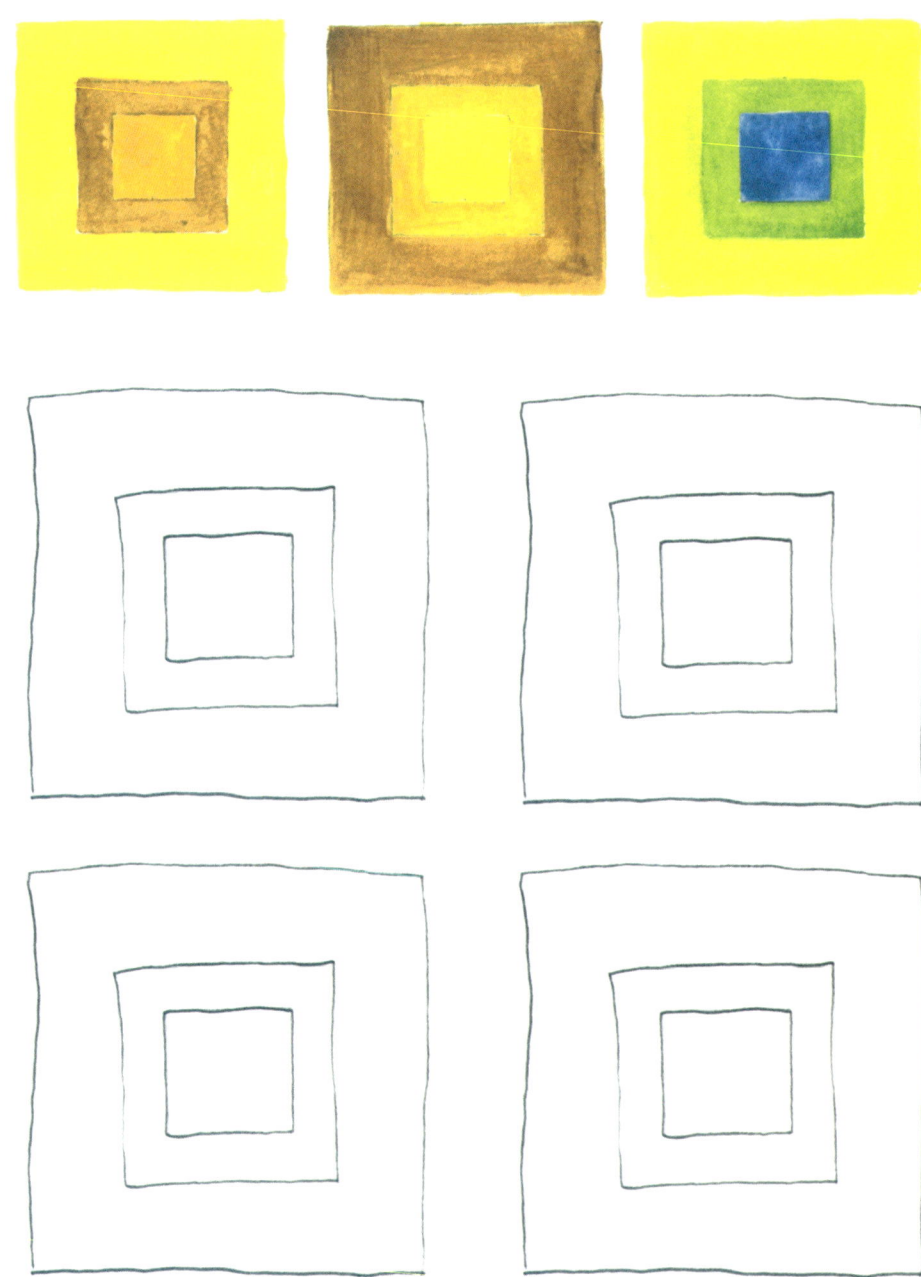

Try your hand at Albers's technique: paint the little interior squares the same color and experiment with different color schemes (complementary, analogous, triatic) for the top and bottom. Does the color shift depending on the surrounding color?

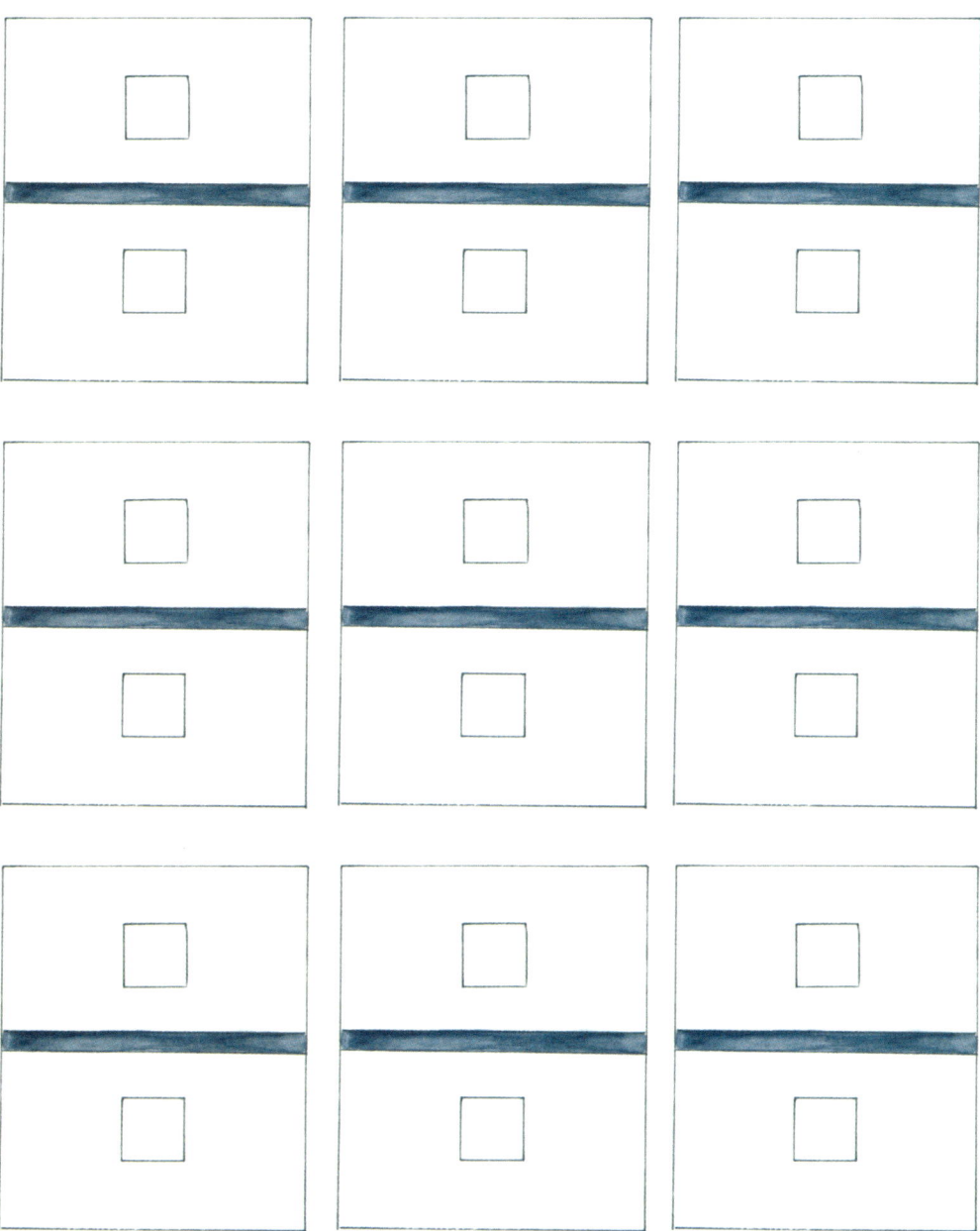

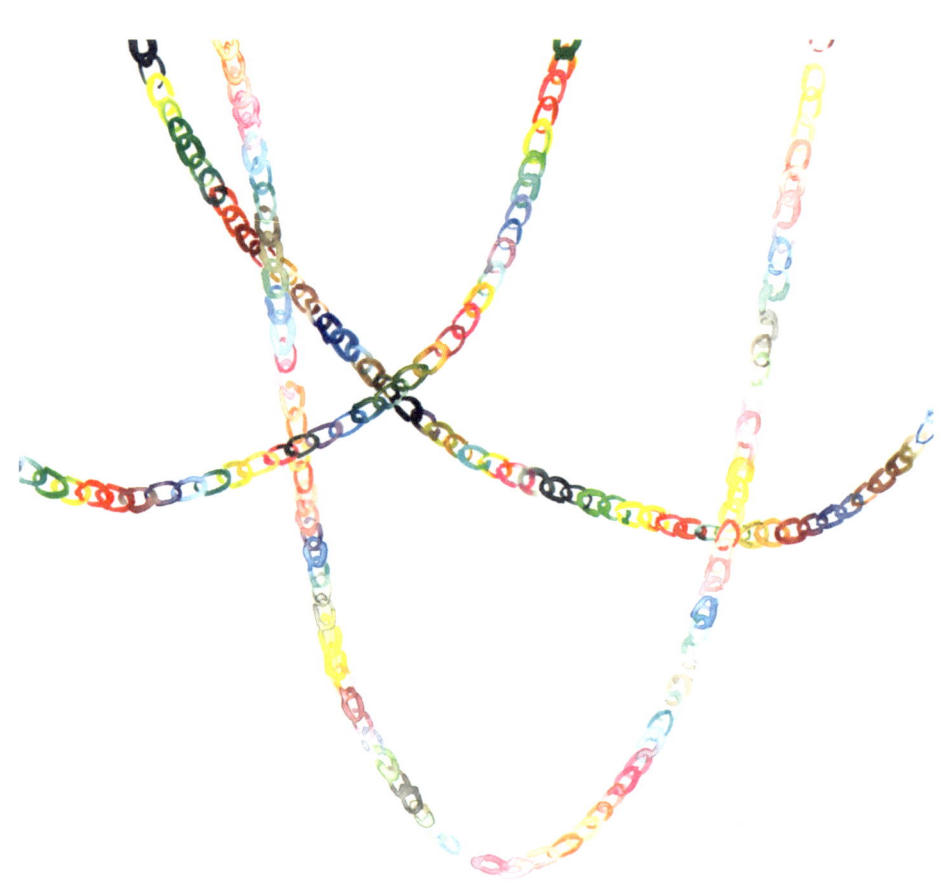

Color Meditation | **WILD CARD**

This is it. You've reached the end of this book and this is our last color meditation together. Although I hope it's not your last color meditation ever. You now know enough about this process to do whatever the heck you want. So make this one weird. Or make it lovely. Or paint while standing on your head. I hope you feel that now, more than ever, the important thing is just to get it done.

► Wild card!

ACKNOWLEDGMENTS

Oh, where to begin? I feel like I owe many people a lot of gratitude.

To my husband Dietrich—Your implicit support of my endeavors, and the continual care and love you provide—immeasurable. It has been an honor to share this life with you. Thank you. I love you.

To my parents—I've said it before, but I'll say it again—you are the kindest (waaaaay nicer than me!) and most supportive parents I've ever met. I can't thank you enough for all that you have done and continue to do. You enrich my life in so many ways, and I'm so grateful that I am your kid.

To S + S (my grandparents)—I wish you were alive to read this, but I can picture the pride that would be on your faces. I always talk about you both and much of who I am is because of you.

To all of my artist, maker, gallerist, crafter colleagues, and friends—If I tried to list you I'm sure I would forget someone and I'd feel awful. So instead I offer this: You know who you are. If we have texted, emailed, lunched, had cocktails, pushed pins into a wall until our fingers hurt, made a thousand holes in the wall, or glued small bits of plastic in rainbow order together, been in a show, laughed or chatted at Craftcation or any other venue, DMd on Insta, commiserated on FB, taught together, made a color wheel together, gone for a walk, drawn together, rolled eyes at something, had a conversation about art/life/love/color, planned/schemed/remembered together, belly-laughed until we cried, or just cried . . . then THANK YOU. Community is so very, very important, and I am blessed to have such a wide-reaching and generous one to call mine. I am forever grateful for your inspiration and cheering me on. You all just being you is a wonder to behold.

I do, though, have to give Susie Ghahremani and Lea Redmond special shout-outs for their titling encouragement and work-shopping.

To Jenn Brown–The moment we spoke about that book that in the end didn't come into being I knew I liked you–immensely. This was only solidified when we met face to face. Your quiet but steadfast and enthusiastic nature is the sail that was needed to guide this ship. Your uncanny ability to simply "get it" has made this process exciting and fun. It has been a joy to collaborate with you and I can't thank you enough for all the guidance, understanding, and advocating.

To everyone at Roost–What a great team! If only everyone had this kind of support, generosity, and professionalism to back them up and physically manifest dreams. Thank you all so much. This literally could not have come to fruition without you.

To all the color enthusiasts and artists of the world–This book is for you. Some people might think it's frivolous to be this preoccupied by color. But we know better. Every time I post/show a color meditation and you respond, I know I'm not alone. When I've taught the technique, I've seen how students are altered. It's hokey, but I sincerely believe art and color can change our lives. It can be a monumental or miniscule shift but it's definitely something, and that makes it all worth it.

RESOURCES

BOOKS

Albers, Josef. *Interaction of Color: 50th Anniversary Edition*. New Haven, CT: Yale University, 2013.

Itten, Johannes. *The Elements of Color*. Hoboken, NJ: John Wiley & Sons, 1970.

Finlay, Victoria. *The Brilliant History of Color in Art*. Los Angeles: Getty Publications, 2014.

Finlay, Victoria. *Color: A Natural History of the Palette*. New York: Random House, 2004.

Goethe, Johann Wolfgang von. *Theory of Colours*. Translated by Charles Lock Eastlake. Cambridge, MA: MIT Press, 1970.

St. Clair, Kassia. *The Secret Lives of Colors*. New York: Penguin, 2017.

Syme, Patrick. *Werner's Nomenclature of Colours: Adapted to Zoology, Botany, Chemistry, Mineralogy, Anatomy, and the Arts*. Washington, DC: Smithsonian Books, 2018.

TOOLS AND SUPPLIES

Adobe Color: color.adobe.com

Adobe's color site is a really fun way to explore color schemes—especially the "Explore" tab, where you can check out schemes that people all over the world have put together.

Color-aid: www.coloraid.com

The velvety, acid-free, practically wrinkle-proof paper has been used in old-school art and design projects for decades. With impeccable consistency Color-aid provides excellent color matching and can be used in lieu of paint for some color theory exercises.

Daniel Smith Watercolors: danielsmith.com/watercolor/

They have 250 different colors on hand—the most of any art supply company.

Holbein: www.holbeinartistmaterials.com/

Another Japanese company, their watercolors and gouaches have a really great consistency and pack a pigment punch. They also have a really cool Acrylic

Gouache paint that feels like a gouache when painting but acts like an acrylic when dry (meaning you can't rewet it).

Kuretake ZIG: kuretakezig.us

One of my favorite watercolor/art suppliers.

Munsell Color: munsell.com/about-munsell-color/how-color-notation-works

In particular, there's a student color set that is really fun to work through.

Pantone: www.pantone.com

If you can't find or pick a color, just grab a Pantone chip book. Pantone just exudes color cool.

Winsor & Newton: www.winsornewton.com/na/shop/water-colour

Founded in 1832 Winsor & Newton has been making quality paint for almost two hundred years!

SHOPS

Arch Art Supplies: squareup.com/store/archsupplies

A San Francisco favorite.

Artist Craftsman Art Stores: www.artistcraftsman.com

There is one close to my house, so I frequent it often. This store has a mom-and-pop feel and excellent variety.

A Case for Making: www.caseformaking.com

A small San Francisco store that makes watercolors and has amazing art supplies.

Dick Blick Art Materials: www.dickblick.com

Dick Blick is the biggest supplier on the block. They have locations nationwide and offer an excellent selection—they offer even more online than they do in stores.

Long Weekend: longweekend.virb.com

A small Oakland, California, store that has an amazing array of eclectic art supplies, including stellar watercolors.

Pigment: http://pigment.tokyo

An *amazing* store in Japan that sells straight pigments as well as watercolors, brushes, etc. Their wall of pigments is one of my personal seven wonders of the world.

ABOUT THE AUTHOR

Lisa Solomon resides in Oakland, California with her husband, daughter, an assortment of oddball rescue pets, a garden, a backyard studio, and a bevy of art supplies including: many, many spools of thread (Gutterman is her favorite), quite a collection of embroidery floss, and enough watercolor to last for the next five years (she hopes). She received her BA in art practice from UC Berkeley, her MFA from Mills College, and has been an Adjunct/Visiting Professor in the Bay Area for over fifteen years. Her layered mixed-media works and grand-sized installations often utilize unconventional mediums, humor, and color to explore gender, identity, and personal histories, as well as the nature of *art* and *craft* itself. She has exhibited internationally in a multitude of venues. As a Hapa (her mother is Japanese, her father Caucasian), she sees hybridity—in materials, in concept—as integral to her practice.

When not focused on her own work, Solomon likes to think she is pushing the next generation of artists to refine their skills, think beyond accepted techniques, and reflect on their own lives, including the potential political ramifications of just *being* an artist/maker in our society. She is profoundly interested in bridging the gaps between being creative, living creatively, *and* making a living as a creative. Learn more at www.lisasolomon.com.

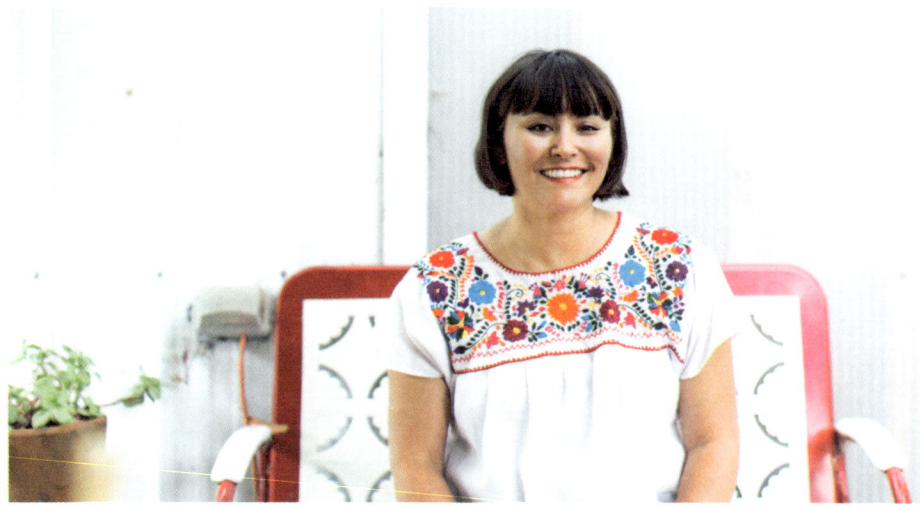

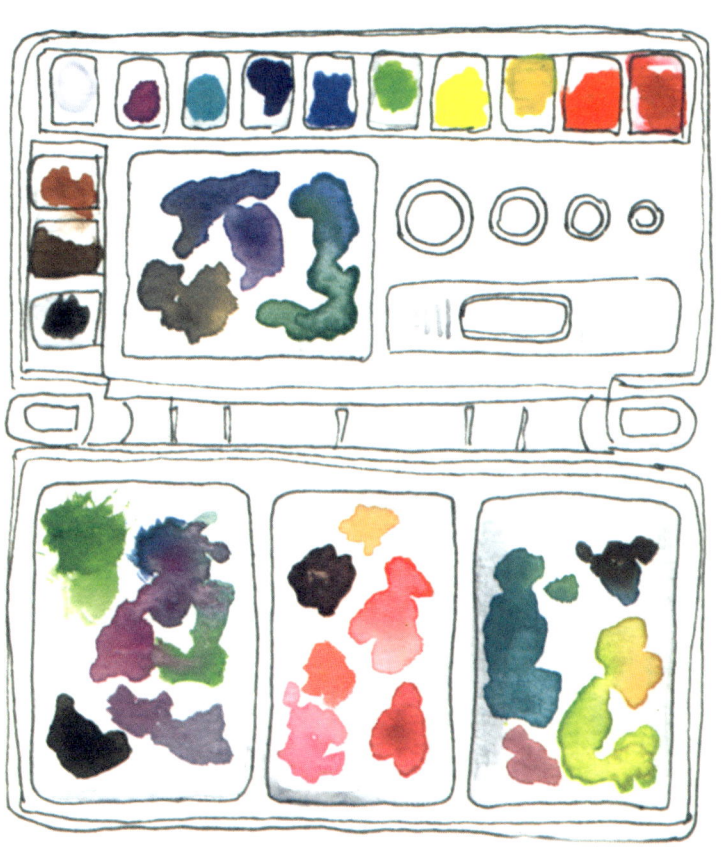

Roost Books
An imprint of Shambhala Publications, Inc.
2129 13th Street
Boulder, Colorado 80302
roostbooks.com

14 13 12 11 10 9 8

Printed in Malaysia

Shambhala Publications makes every effort to print on acid-free, recycled paper. .

Roost Books is distributed worldwide by Penguin Random House, Inc., and its subsidiaries.

Designed by Allison Meierding

Library of Congress Cataloging-in-Publication Data
Names: Solomon, Lisa, author.
Title: A field guide to color: a watercolor workbook / Lisa Solomon.
Description: First edition. | Boulder, Colorado: Roost Books, 2019. | Includes bibliographical references.
Identifiers: LCCN 2018030293 | ISBN 9781611806120 (pbk.: alk. paper)
Subjects: LCSH: Color in art. | Painting–Technique.
Classification: LCC ND1490 .S65 2019 | DDC 752–dc23
LC record available at https://lccn.loc.gov/2018030293